MAKE ROOM
for CHRISTMAS
QUILTS

Holiday Decorating Ideas from Nancy J. Martin

Nancy J. Martin

Martingale™
& COMPANY

CREDITS

President • *Nancy J. Martin*
CEO • *Daniel J. Martin*
Publisher • *Jane Hamada*
Editorial Director • *Mary V. Green*
Managing Editor • *Tina Cook*
Technical Editor • *Karen Costello Soltys*
Copy Editor • *Erana Bumbartadore*
Design Director • *Stan Green*
Illustrator • *Laurel Strand*
Cover and Text Designer • *Trina Stahl*
Photographer • *Brent Kane*

That Patchwork Place® is an imprint of Martingale &
Company™.

Make Room for Christmas Quilts: Holiday Decorating
Ideas from Nancy J. Martin
© 2002 by Nancy J. Martin

Martingale & Company
20205 144th Avenue NE
Woodinville, WA 98072-8478 USA
www.martingale-pub.com

Printed in China
07 06 05 04 03 02   8 7 6 5 4 3 2

MISSION STATEMENT

*We are dedicated to providing quality products
and service by working together to inspire creativity
and to enrich the lives we touch.*

Library of Congress Cataloging-in-Publication Data

Martin, Nancy J.
    Make room for Christmas quilts / holiday decorating
ideas from Nancy J. Martin.
        p. cm.
    ISBN 1-56477-351-5
    1. Patchwork—Patterns. 2. Quilting. 3. Christmas
decorations. 4. Patchwork quilts. I. Title.
TT835 .M3829397 2002
746.46'041—dc21   2002003483

DEDICATION

To Megan Jane Martin, my granddaughter,
who makes every Christmas extra special for me.

ACKNOWLEDGMENTS

Thanks to all of the generous people who contributed their talents to this book.

Alvina Nelson, Sue von Jentzen, and Hazel Montague for their exquisite hand quilting.

Millicent Agnor and her fine Amish quilting service,
including Rachel Hochstetler, Martha Hochstetler, Lydia Mast, and Anna Raber.

Frankie Schmitt of Dizzy Stitches, Becky Krause, Pam Clark, and
Dawn Kelly for delightful machine quilting.

Cleo Nollette, for help with the stitching.

My friends Alice Berg, Sandy Bonsib, Mary Hickey, Sylvia Johnson,
Cleo Nollette, and Mary Ellen Von Holt, who made quilts for this book
and allowed us to photograph their homes.

CONTENTS

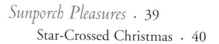

INTRODUCTION

Writing *Make Room for Quilts* a few years ago was one of the most enjoyable experiences I've had as an author because it combined two of my favorite hobbies: decorating and quilting. I redecorate my home often, whether it's with a full-scale makeover or a simple changing of accessories for each season. My favorite time to decorate is Christmas, so it seemed only natural to dedicate an entire book to this special season. It's a time when I pull out all the stops and give each room an added, festive touch.

I often serve as hostess for my quilting group's Christmas party, which is always held in early December. That means I begin decorating my home the day after Thanksgiving in order to have everything ready in time for this kickoff to a month full of festivities. Quilts are an integral part of my decorating scheme, and this special season is the perfect time to display some of my cherished Christmas quilts. I also bring out special collections to share with holiday visitors, such as my blue pottery Santas,

ABOVE: *A light snowfall reflects the soft glow of candles in each window of our colonial-style home.*
OPPOSITE: *The dining room table is set with red-and-white transferware dishes and cranberry goblets for a holiday party. The red-and-white antique "Pine Burr" quilt hung over the cupboard door serves as a perfect backdrop for a festive meal.*

ABOVE: *Pomanders fill the house
with a spicy holiday aroma.*
LEFT: *Ornaments collected
over the years adorn the branches of our
Christmas tree.*

*The dining room is decorated to welcome guests to a Christmas party,
in this case the annual gathering of the Monday Night Bowling League,
my quilting group. Red toile slipcovers camouflage standard folding
chairs and complement the table settings.*

antique children's toys, and my treasured Christmas dinnerware.

Each year I plan a theme for my Christmas decor. I usually begin by searching through my idea files and magazines. Also, I'm heavily influenced by my other hobbies, such as gardening, and because of this I like to use an abundance of herbs, plants, and natural materials in my decorations.

Christmas includes not only wondrous sights of decorated rooms, but also special scents. Whether it's the smell of cookies baking in the oven, paperwhites in bloom, or a freshly cut tree, the holiday season is full of aromas that bring back so many cherished memories. So, in addition to directions for many of my favorite quilts, I've also included instructions for making some of my scented projects that make the season festive.

Christmas is full of symbolism, from trees and wreaths to angels and Santas. One of my favorite symbols to use in Christmas quilts is the home. "Home for Christmas" is a tradition that many hold close to their hearts. It's been the subject of books, poems, and songs. Church services, public celebrations, and parties add to the holiday excitement, but to me, the important celebration is with my family at home, which may be why I so enjoy decorating every room in the house.

Christmas quilts are often red and green, so if you want to incorporate a Christmas quilt into the color scheme of a pastel room, it calls for some ingenuity. Since I have several pastel rooms in my home, I'm sharing my decorating ideas for these somewhat challenging spaces.

Whether you spend Christmas at home amidst Christmas quilts, in a cabin in the woods, or at a ski lodge, remember that Christmas is about an attitude of goodwill, kindness, and sharing. We make gifts to share, prepare special meals, and plan holiday activities to celebrate the true meaning of the season.

MERRY CHRISTMAS,

Nancy J. Martin

ABOVE: *Red-and-white transferware plates—both old and new—grace the dining room table. A centerpiece crafted from fresh holiday greenery contributes to the scents of the season.*
RIGHT: *A profusion of holiday flowers fills the open fireplace when it's not in use and adds a bit of contrast to the "St. Benedict's Star" quilt and cool blue-and-white color scheme.*

PART ONE

CHRISTMAS

AT HOME

A Festive Foyer

The foyer is one of the most important areas to decorate for the holidays. It sets a theme and a festive tone for all who enter. I like to make sure that my holiday decor both looks and smells wonderful, so when you enter my house you'll find pots of paperwhites that provide a heady aroma, white poinsettias that set a rich tone, and a stack of cozy quilts that signify the importance of comfort in our home. Then I add a touch of glitz with sprays of fresh greens tied with silk ribbons and silver ornaments.

I'm fortunate that my foyer has green walls—although they're more of a yellow green than a deep Christmas green. To provide holiday spirit as well as coordinate with the walls, the "Love's Link at Christmas" quilt was made in the perfect shades of green to hang on the wall behind the entry bench.

Antique quilts in cheerful shades of red and green provide a warm and welcoming touch to the holiday decor.

RIGHT: The foyer is filled with wondrous holiday sights and scents: paperwhites in bloom, scented candles, and wreaths and sprays of fresh greens.
OPPOSITE: "Love's Link at Christmas" hangs behind an entryway bench piled with quilts and gaily wrapped presents.

LOVE'S LINK AT CHRISTMAS

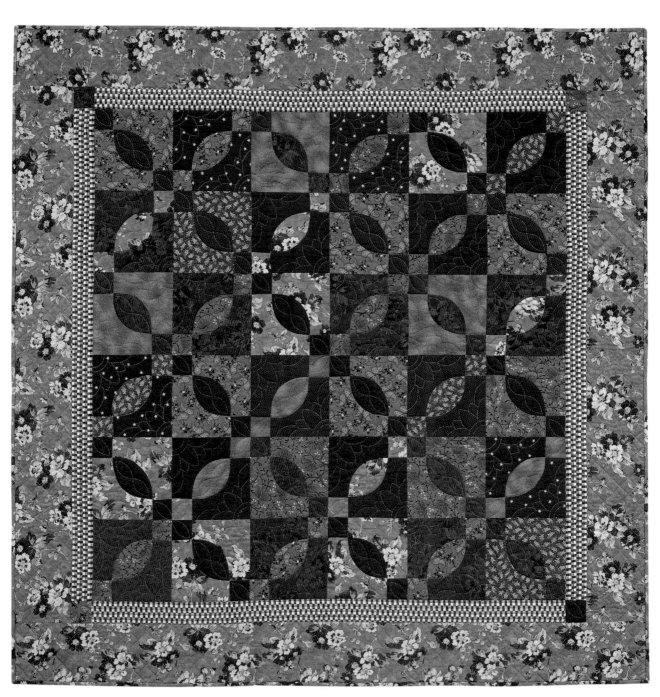

By Nancy J. Martin, Woodinville, Washington, 2001. Quilted by Alvina Nelson, Salina, Kansas.
Finished quilt size: 58½" x 58½"; finished block size: 7¼".

Traditional Lover's Link blocks pieced in a collection of red and green fabrics make this quilt quite a Christmas statement, especially when prominently displayed just inside the door, where the quilt can welcome holiday visitors.

Materials

Yardages are based on 42"-wide fabrics.

+ 1¼ yds. green floral fabric for outer border
+ ½ yd. *each* of five assorted green prints for blocks
+ ½ yd. *each* of five assorted red prints for blocks
+ ½ yd. check for inner border
+ 3¾ yds. fabric for backing
+ ⅝ yd. fabric for bias binding
+ 65" x 65" batting

Cutting

Patterns for pieces A, B, and C are on page 18.

From the assorted green prints, cut:
+ 36 template A
+ 18 template B*
+ 36 template C*

From one green print, cut:
+ 2 squares, 2½" x 2½"

From the assorted red prints, cut:
+ 36 template A
+ 18 template B*
+ 36 template C*

Cut the B and C pieces in pairs so you'll have matching fabrics in each block.

From one red print, cut:
+ 2 squares, 2½" x 2½"

From the check, cut:
+ 5 strips, 2½" x 42"

From the green floral, cut:
+ 6 strips, 5¾" x 42"

Block Assembly

1. Make plastic templates from patterns A, B, and C found on page 18.

2. Pin a green A piece to a red B wedge, carefully matching seam lines at the ends and centers of each piece. Stitch, removing pins as you sew. Press seam allowances toward the wedge. Join a pair of matching red C squares to the short ends of a coordinating green A piece. Press the seam allowances toward the squares.

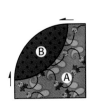
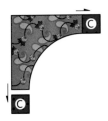

3. Repeat step 2, reversing the placement of the red and green fabrics.

4. Pin the two segments from step 1 together, carefully matching seam lines and center markings. Stitch. Press the seam allowances away from the B fabric to complete Block A. Repeat, making 18 A blocks with green backgrounds.

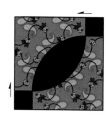

Block A
Make 18.

5. Pin the block segments from step 2 together, carefully matching seam lines and center markings. Stitch. Press the seam allowances away from the B fabric to complete Block B. Repeat, making 18 B blocks with red backgrounds.

Block B
Make 18.

Assembling the Quilt

1. Join six blocks together to form a row, alternating Blocks A and B. Make three rows that begin with Block A and three rows that begin with Block B, being sure to angle the blocks as shown.

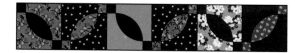

Make 3.

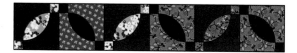

Make 3.

2. Alternating the A and B rows, join them together to form the quilt top, as shown.

Adding the Borders

1. Measure the length and width of your quilt top through the center of your quilt. Sew two of the check inner border strips together end to end, and cut an inner border to the exact length of your quilt top. Sew the leftover portion of the strip to a full-length check strip. Cut another inner border the exact length of your quilt. Sew the remaining two strips together, then sew the leftover portion of the other check strip to one end. Cut two borders the exact length of your quilt top from this strip.

2. Sew two of the inner border strips to the quilt, as shown.

Quilt Plan

3. Sew a 2½" red corner square and a 2½" green corner square to opposite ends of the remaining inner borders.

Make 2.

4. Stitch the top and bottom borders to the quilt top, matching the colors of the corner squares to the adjacent squares on the quilt top.

5. Measure the length of your quilt top through the center, including inner borders. Sew three of the green floral strips together end to end, and cut two outer borders the exact length of your quilt from the long strip. Sew one of the borders to each side of the quilt top, and press the seam allowances toward the green floral fabric.

6. Measure the width of the quilt top through the center, including the side borders you just added. Sew the remaining three green floral strips together end to end, and cut two outer borders to this length. Sew the borders to the top and bottom of the quilt, pressing the seam allowances toward the green floral fabric.

Finishing the Quilt

1. Piece the quilt backing so that it is approximately 6" larger than the quilt top. Layer the backing, batting, and quilt top, and baste, referring to "Layering and Basting" on page 155.

2. Hand or machine quilt your project as desired. The quilt shown has a pumpkin seed design quilted in the four-patch units and half of the same design in the B wedges. Snowflakes (pattern is on page 19) are quilted in the border and then surrounded by a grid pattern. In the large areas where the blocks are joined, you could quilt any medallion or snowflake pattern.

3. Trim the excess batting and backing from the finished quilt. If desired, add a hanging sleeve, referring to page 157 for details.

4. Cut bias strips to make 240" of bias binding and attach it to the quilt, referring to page 157 for instructions.

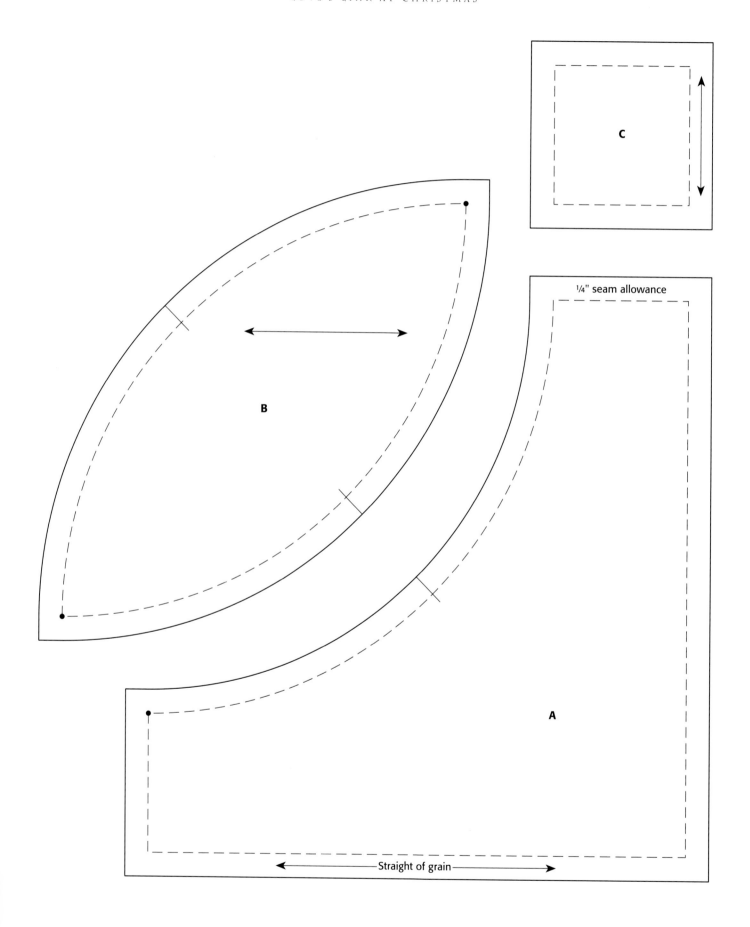

C

¼" seam allowance

B

A

Straight of grain

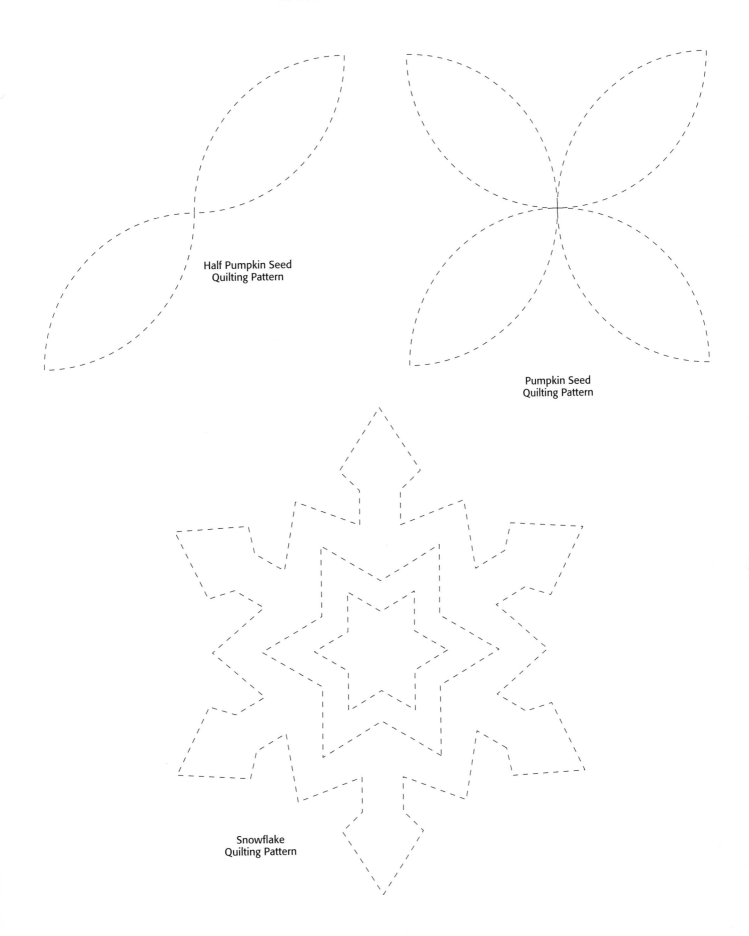

Half Pumpkin Seed
Quilting Pattern

Pumpkin Seed
Quilting Pattern

Snowflake
Quilting Pattern

A ROMANTIC LIVING ROOM

Decorating my living room for the holidays seems like it would be a challenge because of the room's prominent yellow-and-blue color scheme. But actually, the yellow walls prove a perfect foil for my blue-and-white dishes, and they make it easy to display the Santas from my blue Santa collection. I try to keep the Christmas decor simple in this room and not add too much in the way of new themes or colors—a concept you might want to try if you have a room that's not particularly conducive to traditional red-and-green decorations.

To keep the color scheme simple, I display pots of paperwhites, freesias, and amaryllis in blue-and-white bowls and cachepots. Both pink and white poinsettias add a festive touch that says Christmas while also coordinating with the room's color scheme.

We place our main Christmas tree in the living room and decorate it with dozens of ornaments we've collected and crafted over the years. To continue my china collecting theme, I even hang saucers and small plates from the limbs of the tree using small-sized wire plate hangers and ornament hooks.

My "French Feathered Star" quilt serves as the room's focal point. It blends with the blues of the sofa and other room accessories, but the bright bursts of red, the star motif, and the festive French Provençal fabrics add a hearty portion of Christmas flavor.

My house was designed with an open room concept, so my kitchen, dining area, and living room all flow together. Because each area can be seen from the others, it's important to use each room's main color in smaller amounts throughout the adjoining rooms; that way all three rooms don't have to be the same main color, which can become boring. Near the dining area, for instance, the white chairs have red, green, and blue quilts folded over their backs. The reds in these quilts coordinate with the deep raspberry-red walls of the kitchen.

ABOVE: *Small transferware saucers in both blues and reds decorate the tree.*
OPPOSITE: *The "French Feathered Star" quilt rests on a chair beside a tree decorated with silver, white, and blue ornaments. Toile wrapping paper continues the French flavor of the Provençal prints used in the quilt.*

FRENCH FEATHERED STAR

By Nancy J. Martin, Woodinville, Washington, 1995. Quilted by Alvina Nelson, Salina, Kansas.
Finished quilt size: 62⅞" x 62⅞"; finished block size: 14⅝".

I love red, and when I saw these wonderful fabrics in Provence, I knew they were for me! While the blues and bits of yellow in the Provençal fabrics coordinate with my everyday living room decor, the Feathered Star pattern seems to work particularly well during the holiday season. This quilt contains many little bias squares, but if you're up to the challenge, you can make this pattern in whatever fabrics will work with your holiday decor.

Materials

Yardages are based on 42"-wide fabrics unless otherwise noted.

- 1⅞ yds. red print for border
- 1¾ yds. muslin for feather backgrounds
- ⅝ yd. large paisley print for block centers
- ⅝ yd. blue print for sashing
- ½ yd. *each* of three small prints for block backgrounds
- Nine fat quarters of red, blue, and yellow Provençal prints for feathers
- 3⅞ yds. fabric for backing
- ¾ yd. fabric for bias binding
- 70" x 70" batting

Cutting

Patterns for pieces A and B are on page 27.

From *each* of the three small prints, cut:
- 12 squares, 4" x 4" (36 total)
- 3 squares, 8⅞" x 8⅞" (9 total); cut squares twice diagonally to make 36 triangles

From *each* fat quarter of Provençal print, cut:
- 1 rectangle, 11" x 12"

- 4 template A
- 4 template A reverse
- 2 squares, 1⅞" x 1⅞"; cut squares once diagonally to make 4 triangles
- 4 squares, 3" x 3"; cut squares once diagonally to make 8 triangles
- 4 squares, 1⁹⁄₁₆" x 1⁹⁄₁₆"
- 2 squares, 1½" x 1½", for sashing squares (18 total; you'll need 16)

From the paisley print, cut:
- 9 squares, 6" x 6"

From the muslin, cut:
- 9 rectangles, 11" x 12"
- 8 template B
- 36 squares, 1⅞" x 1⅞"; cut squares once diagonally to make 72 triangles

From the blue print, cut:
- 24 strips, 1½" x 14¾"

From the red print, cut:
- 2 strips, 7¾" x 48¾" (on the lengthwise grain)
- 2 strips, 7¾" x 63¼" (on the lengthwise grain)

Making the Blocks

Two sizes of bias squares are used to make this Feathered Star block: 1½" and 1⁹⁄₁₆". While the sizes are very similar, it is important to use the correct size in the appropriate part of the block, or your pieces won't fit. After you cut the different-sized bias square units, keep them in separate, labeled, resealable bags to avoid frustration while piecing. The 1½" bias squares are used to construct the triangle units. The 1⁹⁄₁₆" bias squares are used to make the square corner units.

It will be easier to cut the 1⁹⁄₁₆" bias squares if you mark that measurement on your ruler with masking tape. The correct measurement is exactly halfway between the 1½" and the 1⅝" ruler markings.

Mix and match the background fabrics and Provençal prints to make nine Feathered Star blocks. Use matching prints for the same units of each block, meaning match the feathers, match the triangles, and match the background fabrics. The directions are given for one block because it is easiest to sew this quilt one block at a time.

1. Pair an 11" x 12" rectangle of Provençal print fabric with a same-sized piece of muslin. Lay the rectangles one on top of the other, right sides facing up. Cut 1¾"-wide bias strips, following the directions for bias squares on page 149. *Be sure to press seams open.* Piece and cut 24 bias squares, 1½" x 1½", and 8 bias squares, 1⁹⁄₁₆" x 1⁹⁄₁₆". Separate, bag, and label your squares.

Cut bias squares from assembled fabric.

2. Sew one 1⅞" muslin triangle and three 1½" bias squares together to make a row, taking care to position the pieces as shown. Press the seam by the single muslin triangle open. Press the remaining seams to one side. Make four of these units.

Make 4.

3. Sew a 1⅞" muslin triangle and three 1½" bias squares together to make a row. Notice that the fabrics are positioned differently than they were in step 2. Sew a 1⅞" Provençal print triangle to the end of the row, as shown. Press the seam by the single muslin triangle open. Press the remaining seams to one side. Make four of these units.

Make 4.

NOTE: *In steps 4–6, you will be sewing partial seams when piecing the triangle units. These seams will be completed as the block is assembled.*

4. Stitch a unit from step 2 to the *left* short side of each large background print triangle, sewing a partial seam, as shown. Press the seam toward the large triangle. Make four of these units.

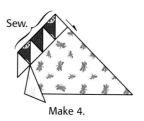

Sew.

Make 4.

5. Repeat to sew a unit from step 3 to the *right* short side of each unit from step 4, sewing a partial seam, as shown; press toward the large triangle.

Make 4.

6. Sew a 3" Provençal print triangle (one that contrasts with the feather fabric) to each short side of the four units made in step 5. Press the seams toward the Provençal print triangles.

7. Sew a Provençal print A diamond to a muslin B triangle, matching notches. Press this seam open. Join this unit to a 1⅜16" bias square to make a row. Repeat to make four identical rows. Press.

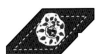

Make 4.

8. Sew a Provençal print A reverse diamond to a muslin B triangle, matching notches, and join the unit to a 1⅜16" bias square. Complete the row by adding a 1⅜16" Provençal print square, as shown. Repeat to make four identical rows, noting that the triangles face in the opposite direction than in the rows made in step 7.

Make 4.

9. Sew a unit from step 7 to the top edge of each 4" small print square, as shown. Press the seam toward the square. Repeat to make four of these units.

Make 4.

10. Sew the units from step 8 to the right edge of each unit made in step 9; press seams away from the square. Make four of these corner squares.

Make 4.

Yellow walls and light furnishings tie together the living, dining, and kitchen areas of the house. The "Feathered World without End" quilt, featuring more Provençal prints and blue toile fabric, hangs above the sofa.

11. Sew a triangle unit from step 6 between two corner square units from step 10. Finish sewing the partial seams, matching the diamond and triangle points. Press the seams toward the triangle unit. Make two of these units.

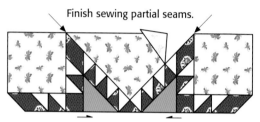

Finish sewing partial seams.

Make 2.

12. Sew a 6⅛" paisley print square between the remaining triangle units from step 6, as shown. Finish sewing the partial seams, matching the diamond and triangle points. Press the seams toward the triangle units. Sew the rows together and press the row seam allowances toward the block center.

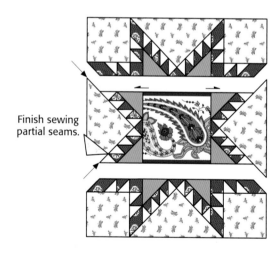

Finish sewing partial seams.

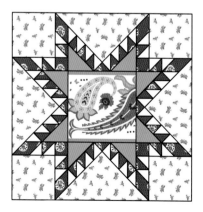

13. Repeat steps 1–12 to make eight more blocks.

Assembling the Quilt

1. Arrange the blocks in three rows of three blocks each, varying the placement of the background fabrics and Provençal prints.

2. Stitch the blocks together in rows, separated by blue sashing strips. Sew a sashing strip to each end of each row. Make three rows.

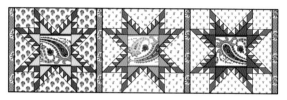

Make 3 rows.

3. Stitch three sashing strips and four 1½" sashing squares together into a row. Repeat to make four sashing rows.

Make 4 rows.

4. Join the rows together, alternating the rows of quilt blocks with the rows of sashing strips.

Adding the Borders

1. Stitch the red print side borders to the quilt top. Press the seams toward the red borders.

2. Stitch the red print top and bottom borders to the quilt top. Press the seams toward the borders.

Finishing the Quilt

1. Piece the quilt backing so that it is approximately 6" larger than the quilt top. Layer the backing, batting, and quilt top, and baste, referring to "Layering and Basting" on page 155.

2. Hand or machine quilt your project as desired. One possibility would be to quilt the Feathered Star blocks in the ditch and accent the wide border with a quilted feather design.

3. Trim the excess batting and backing from the finished quilt. If desired, add a hanging sleeve, referring to page 157 for details.

4. Cut enough bias strips to make 270" of bias binding. Bind the edges, referring to "Binding" on page 157 for instructions.

Quilt Plan

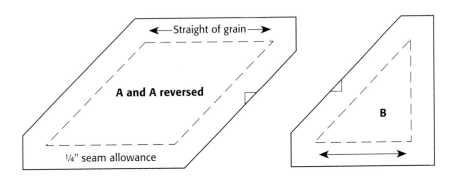

YULETIDE DINING

It's fun to use a special table runner just for the holidays, especially this one, which features one of my favorite techniques—redwork embroidery. It really enhances the table setting and makes holiday meals and buffets more festive. My dining area is not a formal dining room (something I found that I rarely used in my previous homes). Instead we have one large room, about 15 feet by 35 feet, that encompasses both the living room and dining areas.

The dining table takes up a small amount of room without the leaves, but it can expand to seat ten or twelve. Using a smaller table frees up space for a cozy seating area near the window seat. Lightweight chairs and an ottoman are easy to move, so this area can hold an additional table and chairs for large dinner parties.

Holiday greenery and cranberry glass goblets complement the fresh red-and-white color scheme used on the table.

ABOVE RIGHT: *Beyond the dining room table, the window seat with a "Lost Ships" quilt creates a cozy spot to read and relax.*
Blue-and-white quilts stacked atop an antique cupboard filled with blue-and-white dishes help draw the eye upward.
More dishes, collected from French bistros, perch on the ledge above the window seat.
OPPOSITE: *A redwork table runner spreads Christmas cheer at a holiday open house.*

REDWORK TABLE RUNNER
WITH CRAZY QUILT BORDER

By Nancy J. Martin, Woodinville, Washington, 2001.
Finished table runner size: 18" x 31½"; finished block size: 4½".

Beautiful redwork embroidery is surrounded by quick-and-easy foundation-pieced border blocks in this charming holiday table topper. Mix and match scraps or leftover strips to crazy-piece the blocks. They don't have to be Christmas-theme fabrics. Checks, stripes, dots—any red-and-white prints will do. The redwork embroidery alone will proclaim this to be a special-occasion table runner.

Materials

Yardages are based on 42"-wide fabrics unless otherwise noted.

- ⅜ yd. tightly woven white cotton, suitable for embroidery
- ½ yd. muslin for Crazy-Patch foundations
- 1½ yds. *total* assorted scraps of light and dark red prints for border blocks
- ½ yd. red check for bias binding
- ¾ yd. fabric for backing
- 22" x 35" batting
- 3 skeins red embroidery floss
- Red transfer pencil or transfer pen

Redwork Embroidery

1. From the white embroidery fabric, cut a 12" x 25" rectangle. Fold the fabric in half crosswise, and crease to mark the center. Using a transfer pencil, trace the pinecone design on page 36 onto one-half of the embroidery fabric, referring to the illustra-

tion for placement. Rotate the design 180° and transfer the design to the other half of the fabric.

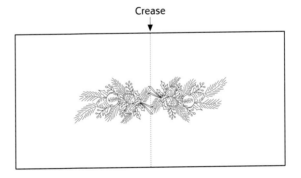

The redwork table runner sets the stage for a holiday cookie exchange.

2. Transfer the "Have Yourself a Merry Little Christmas" design on page 37 to each long edge of the embroidery fabric, centering it evenly about 1¼" away from the center design, as indicated in the illustration below.

3. Transfer the "Glory to God" and poinsettia designs on page 36 to each short edge of the embroidery fabric, referring to the illustration for placement.

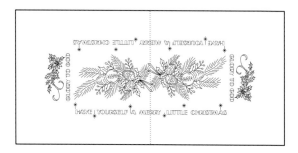

Two comfortable chairs and an ottoman provide a relaxing area near the window seat. The red-and-white "Lost Ships" signature quilt adds a touch of holiday sparkle.

4. Embroider all parts of the design using two strands of floss and a simple outline stitch, with the following exceptions: use French knots in the centers of the poinsettias, and fill in all berries with the satin stitch.

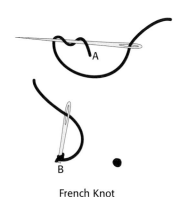

French Knot

Outline Stitch

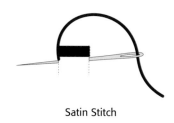

Satin Stitch

5. Place the completed stitchery on a clean, thick, white towel, right side facing down. Press the completed stitchery from the wrong side.

6. Trim the completed piece to measure 9½" x 23", making sure the design is evenly centered.

Crazy-Patch Foundation Border

1. From muslin, cut 18 squares, 6" x 6", for foundation piecing of border blocks.

2. From the assorted light and dark red prints, cut 18 Crazy-Patch center pieces, using the five-sided template on page 37.

3. Place a Crazy-Patch center, right side up, in the middle of a muslin square.

4. Using a scrap of fabric with a straight edge, align the next piece of fabric, right sides down, along one edge of the center piece. Make sure the scrap you're adding is at least ½" longer than the edge of the center piece.

5. Stitch the fabrics to the foundation using a ¼" seam. Flip over the top fabric and finger-press it in place. Trim away the excess fabric to form a straight edge that extends from the adjacent side of the center fabric.

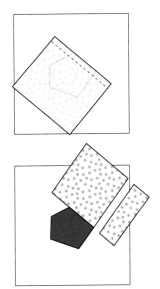

Trim excess fabric.

6. Align a scrap of a different fabric with the long straight edge created by the first two fabrics; stitch as in step 5. Trim away excess fabric to form a straight edge that aligns with the next side of the center fabric.

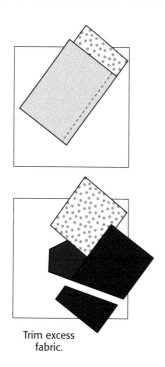

Trim excess fabric.

7. Continue adding scraps in the same manner until all of the muslin foundation is covered. Remember to place the scraps so that a new straight edge will be created each time.

Crazy Patch Border Block

8. When all 18 foundation squares are completed, trim each one to measure 5" x 5".

Adding the Border

For this project, the borders are added to the layered embroidery, batting, and backing. That way, no stitching in the ditch will be visible from the top of the completed table runner.

1. Cut the batting and backing fabric to measure 22" x 35".

2. Layer the batting on top of the wrong side of the backing fabric.

3. Center the completed embroidery on top of the batting. Pin, and then baste the layers to hold them in place while adding the border. Mark the center point of the long edge of the embroidery.

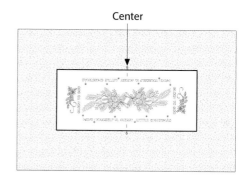

Center

4. Stitch five Crazy-Patch blocks together using a ¼" seam allowance. Press the seam allowances open. Make two of these borders.

Border
Make 2.

34

5. Mark the center of each border. Pin a border to one long edge of the stitchery, right sides together and centers aligned. Stitch using a ¼" seam allowance, as shown. Flip the border open so that all right sides are facing up. Press, taking care around the exposed batting areas, especially if you're using a polyester batting. Repeat for the remaining long border.

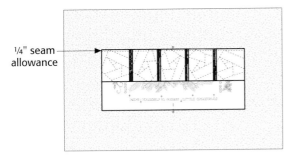

¼" seam allowance

6. Stitch four Crazy-Patch blocks together and press the seam allowances open. Make two of these end borders.

7. Sew the end borders to the short edges of embroidery, right sides together and aligning seams. Flip open the border so that all right sides are facing up. Press.

Finishing the Table Runner

1. With a rotary cutter and a ruler, trim away the excess batting and backing, and square up the edges of the table runner, if necessary. Baste around the perimeter of the table runner to hold the layers together.

2. Cut bias strips from the red check fabric to make 110" of bias binding and attach it to the table runner, referring to "Binding" on page 157 for more details.

   NOTE: *This is a decorative table runner and won't be washed. If you plan to use yours more heavily and would like to make sure it's washable, you can add quilting in the ditch around the Crazy-Patch blocks. To protect your project from stains you might want to treat it with Scotchgard so that drips or spills will bead up and can be blotted away.*

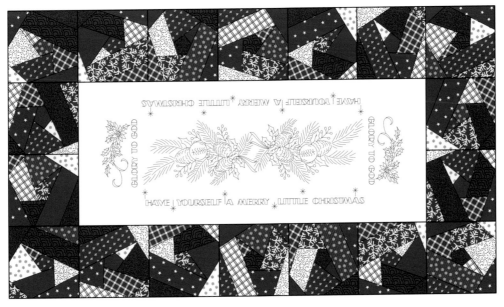

Quilt Plan

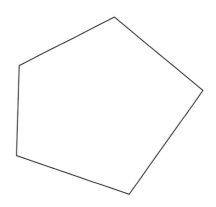

HAVE YOURSELF A MERRY

MERRY LITTLE CHRISTMAS

SUNPORCH PLEASURES

I fondly remember the long, narrow sunporch attached to one side of my grandmother's house. It was an unheated space, but it had plenty of windows that let in both light and warmth. I wanted to create the same type of nostalgic space when I added a sunporch to the side of our house.

Our sunporch runs across one entire side of the house and has French doors opening into both the living room and the dining area. A space like this is fun to decorate, especially during the holidays. Normally, my sunporch is decorated in a yellow-and-blue color scheme, echoing the colors used in the main living areas but a few shades lighter. However, it's easier—and more fun—to change the colors to a splashy red-and-green theme in this area for the holidays.

Freshly cut evergreens are hung around the door frame, and bright red poinsettias and kalanchoe, a succulent plant, add a spark of color. We overcame the challenge of decorating a long, narrow space such as a porch by dividing the room into separate areas. On my porch, I've used a small table and chairs at one end to serve as a breakfast room. Here, vintage fabric was used to make the tablecloth and chair pads. A folding screen, draped with a quilt, helps screen the sun's rays. During the holiday season, my "Star-Crossed Christmas" quilt makes its home on the screen.

A second seating area at the other end of the sunporch features a comfortable loveseat and a simple garden chair. My favorite "Rose Wreath" quilt hangs on the brick wall between these two areas, fronted by pots of paperwhites.

TOP: *The "Rose Wreath" quilt provides a pretty backdrop for pots of paperwhites and a collection of homemade Santas.*
ABOVE: *Vintage fabrics are a perfect decorating choice for a sunporch. These fruit fabrics are a great addition at Christmas with their predominately red, green, and white color palette.*
OPPOSITE: *The "Star-Crossed Christmas" quilt is the focal point of holiday decoration on the sunporch.*

STAR-CROSSED CHRISTMAS

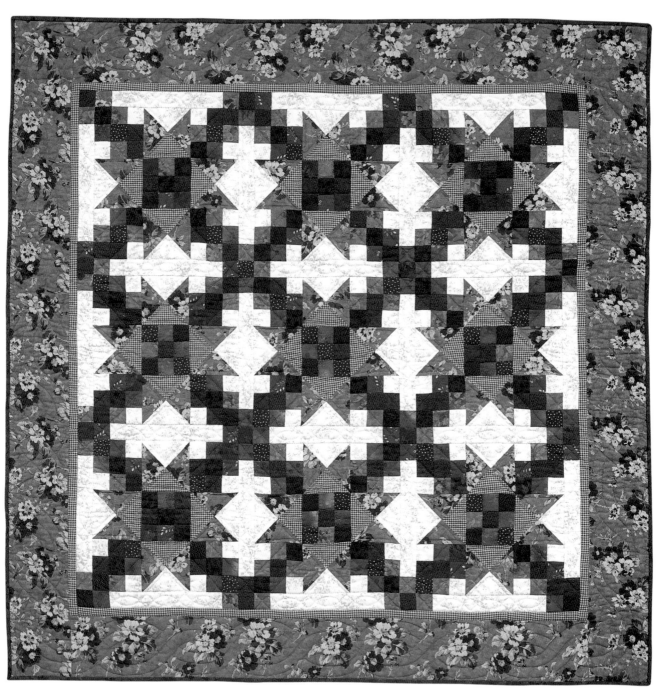

By Nancy J. Martin, Woodinville, Washington, 2001. Quilted by Rachel Hochstetler, Marion, Wisconsin.
Finished quilt size: 60" x 60"; finished block size: 13½".

Holiday reds and greens mingle merrily in this diagonal chain quilt. The chain is created by carefully arranging the red and green patches in the nine-patch units that are used for the corners and centers of each large Star block. A large border print surrounds the quilt and is also used for the star points to unify the design.

Materials

Yardages are based on 42"-wide fabrics unless otherwise noted.

+ 3 yds. light background for blocks
+ 2 yds. green floral print for stars and outer border
+ ½ yd. red check for blocks and inner border
+ 1 fat quarter *each* of five assorted red prints for nine-patch units
+ 1 fat quarter *each* of five assorted green prints for nine-patch units
+ 3⅔ yds. fabric for backing
+ ½ yd. red print for bias binding
+ 66" x 66" batting

Cutting

From the light background, cut:
+ 4 strips, 2" x 42"; cut in half to make 8 strips, 2" x 21"
+ 9 squares, 5¾" x 5¾"; cut squares twice diagonally to make 36 triangles
+ 24 strips, 2" x 11"

From *each* red print, cut:
+ 4 strips, 2" x 21" (20 total; you'll only need 17)
+ 2 squares, 2" x 2" (10 total; you'll only need 8)

From *each* green print, cut:
+ 5 strips, 2" x 21" (25 total; you'll only need 22)
+ 7 squares, 2" x 2" (35 total; you'll only need 32)

From the red check, cut:
+ 5 strips, 1½" x 42", for the inner border
+ 9 squares, 5¾" x 5¾"; cut squares twice diagonally to make 36 triangles

From the green floral, cut:
+ 2 strips, 6" x 49½", for outer borders (on the lengthwise grain)
+ 2 strips, 6" x 60", for outer borders (on the lengthwise grain)
+ 2 strips, 2" x 42"; cut strips in half to make four 2" x 21" strips
+ 18 squares, 5¾" x 5¾"; cut squares twice diagonally to make 36 triangles

ABOVE LEFT: *A collection of children's toys and a garden chair covered with vintage cushions and pillows make a charming corner at the far end of the sunporch.*
ABOVE RIGHT: *The seating area of the sunporch includes a sofa slipcovered patchwork-style with a blend of new and vintage fabrics. The "Kitty Homemaker" redwork quilt folded over the back of the sofa strengthens the nostalgic flavor of the sunporch.*

Making the Nine-Patch Units

1. Sew a 2"-wide red strip to either side of a 2"-wide green strip. Press the seam allowances toward the green strip. Repeat to make two of these strip sets. Cut the strip sets into eighteen 2"-wide segments.

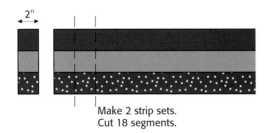

Make 2 strip sets.
Cut 18 segments.

2. Sew a 2"-wide green strip to either side of a 2"-wide red strip. Press the seam allowances toward the green strips. Cut the strip set into nine 2"-wide segments.

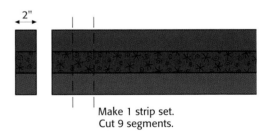

Make 1 strip set.
Cut 9 segments.

3. Sew the segments together as shown to complete nine nine-patch units for the centers of the Star blocks.

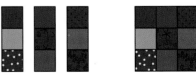

Make 9.

4. Using the 2" red, green, and light background strips, sew a red strip to one side of a green strip and a light strip to the opposite side, as shown. Repeat to make eight red-green-light strip sets. Press the seam allowances toward the green fabric. Cut the strip sets into 72 segments, 2" wide.

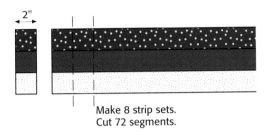

Make 8 strip sets.
Cut 72 segments.

5. Sew a 2"-wide green strip to either side of a 2"-wide red strip. Repeat to make four strip sets. Press the seam allowances toward the green strips. Cut the strip sets into 36 segments, 2" wide.

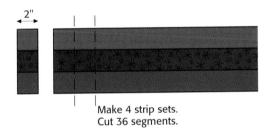

Make 4 strip sets.
Cut 36 segments.

6. Join the segments from steps 4 and 5 to make 36 nine-patch units for the Star block corners. Be sure to flip the segments with the light background pieces so that the segments on the left have the light background in the bottom corner and the segments on the right have the light background in the top corner.

Make 36.

Making the Star Points

1. To make the triangle star points, sew half of the green floral triangles to the red check triangles, as shown. Sew the remaining green floral triangles to the light background triangles, as shown.

2. Sew the pairs of triangles together so that you have two green floral triangles, one light background, and one red check triangle in each unit.

Assembling the Star Blocks

1. Sew the red, green, and light background nine-patch units to either side of a star point unit, making sure that each unit is oriented as shown. Make 18 of these rows.

Make 18.

2. For the center rows of the blocks, sew the star point units to either side of a red-and-green nine-patch unit. Make sure the red triangles are facing the nine-patch units, as shown. Make nine of these rows.

Make 9.

3. Sew the rows together to complete nine Star blocks. Make sure the red-check triangles are facing toward the center of the block, as shown.

Star Block
Make 9.

Assembling the Quilt

1. Sew a 2" green square to each end of 12 of the 2" x 11" light background sashing strips. Press the seam allowances toward the green fabrics.

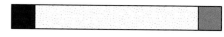

Make 12.

2. Sew three Star blocks and four sashing strips together to make a row, as shown. Repeat to make three rows. Press the seam allowances toward the sashing.

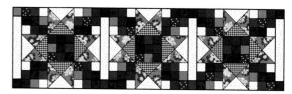

Make 3 rows.

3. Join the remaining 2"-wide red and green strips together, with the green strips on either side of the red strip. Press the seam allowances toward the green strips. Cut eight 2"-wide segments from the strip set.

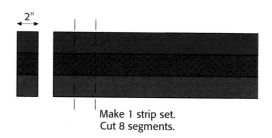

Make 1 strip set.
Cut 8 segments.

When not decorated for the holidays, the sunporch features a sedate yellow-and-blue color scheme.
Here, blue-and-white transferware dishes are a fun addition to the decor.

4. Stitch together three 2" x 11" light background sashing strips and two red-and-green sashing units made in step 3. Press the seam allowances toward the green fabrics. Sew 2" green and red squares to each end of all rows, with the red squares on the very end. Repeat to make four rows.

Make 4 rows.

5. Join the rows of blocks and the sashing strips to assemble the quilt top.

Adding the Borders

1. Cut one of the 1½" red check strips into four equal pieces. Sew one of these short segments onto each of the remaining four red check strips. Trim two of the resulting strips to 47" long for the side borders, and the other two strips to 49½" long for the top and bottom borders. Sew the side inner borders to the quilt top and press the seam allowances toward the borders. Repeat with the top and bottom borders.

2. Stitch the 49½" green floral outer borders to each side of the quilt top. Press the seam allowances toward the outer borders. Sew the 60" green floral borders to the top and bottom of the quilt top, and press the seam allowances toward the outer borders.

Quilt Plan

Finishing the Quilt

1. Piece the quilt backing so that it's approximately 6" larger than the quilt top. Layer the quilt top, batting, and backing, and baste, referring to "Layering and Basting" on page 155.

2. Hand or machine quilt as desired. One possibility is to stitch ¼" inside the triangle shapes, then quilt a diagonal grid through the center and corner nine patches. To emphasize the chain aspect of the quilt pattern, a delicate cable is a good choice for the sashing strips, with a larger cable design stitched in the outer border.

3. Trim the excess batting and backing fabric from the quilt. If desired, add a hanging sleeve, referring to page 157 for details.

4. Cut bias strips to make 250" of bias binding and attach it to the quilt, referring to "Binding" on page 157 for details.

ABOVE LEFT: *Christmas dishes and white poinsettias shine in the sunporch.*
ABOVE RIGHT: *Bottles of colorful peppers look festive against a background of Christmas greenery.*

CHRISTMAS RED FOR THE MASTER BEDROOM

Most people might hesitate to use an energizing color like red in a bedroom, but I find it a wonderful antidote to the gray Seattle mornings. When using a strong color in your decorating, you can offset its potential to be overpowering by also using lots of white. In this case, the woodwork and walls were painted in two complementary shades of white and balanced by an off-white carpet. The effect of this red-and-white color scheme is quite uplifting and perfect for holiday decorating.

I redecorated this room as a personal retreat for myself at a time when we had four generations of family living in the same house. On days when I was feeling too much togetherness with my one-year-old granddaughter or my eighty-something father-in-law, this comfortable room offered a great getaway. A cup of tea and some hand stitchery could always soothe my jangled nerves.

A variety of red check and toile fabrics combine to give the room a sophisticated look that I softened by stitching antique pieces of redwork into pillows and shams. Rather than use a formal window treatment, I tacked lace tablecloths to the window corners and softened the head of the bed by draping an antique piece of lace over the top rail.

The red-and-white quilts and fabrics offered the perfect backdrop for my red-and-white transferware collection, which was overflowing from my kitchen. There's no rule in decorating that says dishes are only for the kitchen and dining room.

It's easy to add some holiday accents to a red-and-white room, such as arrangements of fresh greens and fragrant freesia, or wrapped gifts. Since I wrapped some of my presents in red toile wrapping paper, this room is the perfect place to store them until Christmas morning. Even if your master bedroom doesn't start with a backdrop of red and white, you can add these festive touches to bring a Christmas spirit into your bedroom.

ABOVE: *Antique redwork has been crafted into decorative pillow shams.*
OPPOSITE: *"Aunt Sukey's Christmas Quilt," with its vivid red and green fabrics, provides a lively accent in this red-and-white master bedroom. The "Tree of Life" quilt is folded at the foot of the bed.*

AUNT SUKEY'S
CHRISTMAS QUILT

By Nancy J. Martin, Woodinville, Washington, 2000. Quilted by Lydia Mast, Kenton, Ohio.
Finished quilt size: 52½" x 66½"; finished block size: 12".

Aunt Sukey's Choice is one of my all-time-favorite quilt patterns, and making a special Christmas version makes it all the more endearing to me. This pattern provides the perfect opportunity to use up scraps of red and white fabrics—or splurge and buy some new ones to add a festive touch to your quilt.

Materials

Yardages are based on 42"-wide fabrics unless otherwise noted.

- 1¾ yds. red Christmas print for border
- 1 fat quarter *each* or scraps of six assorted light background prints for bias squares, sashing, and blocks
- 1 fat quarter *each* or scraps of six assorted green prints for bias squares
- 1 fat quarter *each* or scraps of six assorted red prints for blocks and sashing
- 3½ yds. fabric for backing
- ⅝ yd. fabric for bias binding
- 58" x 72" batting

Cutting

From *each* light background print, cut:
- 4 squares, 7" x 7" (24 total)
- 6 strips, 2½" x 12½"
  (36 total; you'll only need 31)
- 16 squares, 2½" x 2½" (96 total)

From *each* red print, cut:
- 28 squares, 2½" x 2½" (168 total; you'll only need 164)

From *each* green print, cut:
- 4 squares, 7" x 7" (24 total)

From red Christmas print, cut:
- 4 strips, 4½" x length of fabric

Block Assembly

1. Pair each 7" green square with a 7" square of light background print. Lay the squares one on top of the other, right sides facing up. Cut 2½"-wide strips on the diagonal, following the directions for bias squares on page 149. Piece and cut a total of 192 bias squares, each 2½" x 2½".

2. Join four red squares to make a four-patch unit. Join two bias squares together as shown for each side of the four-patch unit. Stitch the bias square pairs to the four-patch unit.

3. Make two additional bias square units as you did in step 2. Join a red square to each end of both units. Join the units to those made in step 2.

4. Make four additional bias square units, only this time, join the green triangles together in the center. Sew a light background square to each end of all the units as shown. Then sew a red square to each end of two of the units.

Make 2.

Make 2.

A folding screen with red-and-white toile fabric panels softens a corner with several awkward angles while providing a backdrop for the small tabletop items.

5. Sew the units made in step 4 to the block centers to complete an Aunt Sukey's Choice block, as shown. Repeat to make 12 blocks.

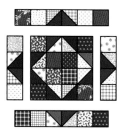 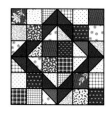

Make 12.

Assembling the Quilt

1. Join three blocks and four sashing strips to make a row. Repeat to make four rows.

Make 4.

2. Join three sashing strips and four red squares to make a sashing row. Repeat to make five sashing rows.

Make 5.

3. Join the rows together to assemble the quilt top, alternating the sashing and block rows.

Adding the Border

1. Measure the length of your quilt top through the center, and trim two of the 4½"-wide border strips to this length. Sew the strips to the sides of the quilt top and press the seam allowances toward the borders.

2. Measure the width of your quilt top through the center and trim the remaining two border strips to this length. Sew the border strips to the top and bottom of the quilt. Press the seam allowances toward the borders.

Quilt Plan

Finishing the Quilt

1. Piece the backing fabric (the yardage allows for the backing to be pieced with a horizontal seam), and trim the backing to about 58" x 72". Layer the backing, bat-

ting, and quilt top, and baste, referring to "Layering and Basting" on page 155.

2. Hand or machine quilt your project as desired. The quilt shown was quilted in the ditch around the center four-patch units with diagonal lines in each corner of the block. The border is quilted with a cable design.

3. Trim the excess batting and backing fabric from the quilt. If desired, add a hanging sleeve, referring to page 157 for details.

4. Cut bias strips to make 245" of bias binding and attach it to the quilt, referring to "Binding" on page 157 for details.

The large master bedroom has a seating area where one can relax and do hand stitchery. A ledge on top of the wainscoting provides display space for my ever-growing collection of red-and-white transferware plates. They can easily be removed and whisked through the dishwasher for use at large gatherings. The "Christmas Nine Patch" quilt finds a perfect resting place on the back of the sofa.

POTTING SHED FUN

My potting shed gives me hours of pleasure, no matter what the season. It's the perfect place for wreath making, forcing bulbs, or arranging holiday flowers. And because I spend so much time in my potting shed, I really wanted it to be decorated.

From the vintage porcelain sink (purchased at a salvage yard for $35 and complete with a drainboard that is a perfect place for potting plants) to the utilitarian potting benches to the bead board paneling on the walls, the inside of my potting shed is both practical and fun. It is also a wonderful spot to stack my collection of 1950s tablecloths and other nostalgic collectibles, which set the theme for the decor.

The decor really came into focus, though, when I began collecting 1940s and 1950s dishes and vases to display on the ledge above the windows. The windows now sport valances made of vintage fabric, and a red farm table sits on an old-fashioned, linoleum-look floor. But when Christmas comes, I can still find room for a small tree and pots of fragrant bulbs.

The "Christmas Bulbs" quilt (opposite and on page 56) was made especially for my potting shed, which I get to enjoy all season long as I'm busy working on other holiday decorations. Even if you don't have a potting shed, this charming little project will be the perfect accent for a kitchen, a mudroom, a hallway, or anyplace else you want to be reminded of your other favorite hobby!

ABOVE LEFT: *Garden ornaments on a small tree add a holiday touch.*
ABOVE RIGHT: *The work table in the potting shed is the perfect place to craft wreaths, swags, and holiday arrangements.*
OPPOSITE: *The "Christmas Bulbs" quilt brightens up the red-and-green color scheme of the potting shed, while paperwhites and freesias scent the air with their wonderful fragrances.*

CHRISTMAS BULBS

By Nancy J. Martin, Woodinville, Washington, 2001. Quilted by Frankie Schmitt, Kenmore, Washington.
Finished quilt size: 53½" x 53½"; finished block size: 11".

Cheery watering cans decked out in Christmas red mingle with bright pots of paper-whites, my favorite seasonal flower. If you've never forced these bulbs to bloom in time for the holidays, pot up a bunch this year and enjoy their lovely fragrance. For even quicker and more enduring results, use fusible web to appliqué paperwhites to a quilt that you can enjoy year after year.

Materials

Yardages are based on 42"-wide fabrics unless otherwise noted.

- 2¼ yds. floral stripe for sashing
- 1 fat quarter *each* of seven assorted background prints for the blocks
- 1 fat eighth *each* of seven assorted red prints for the blocks
- 1 fat eighth *each* of seven assorted green prints for the blocks
- Scraps of white for Paperwhite blocks
- 3½ yds. fabric for backing
- ⅝ yd. fabric for binding
- 59" x 59" batting
- 2 yds. fusible web

Cutting

Patterns for pieces A and B are on page 61. All appliqué patterns are on page 62.

From one background fabric, cut:

- 2 squares, 12" x 12"

From *each* background fabric, cut:

- 2 squares, 1⅞" x 1⅞" (14 total); cut squares once diagonally to make 28 triangles

- 1 square, 1½" x 1½" (7 total)
- 2 rectangles, 1½" x 2½" (14 total)
- 1 template A (7 total)
- 1 template B (7 total)
- 1 rectangle, 1½" x 4½" (7 total)
- 1 rectangle, 3½" x 6½" (7 total)
- 1 rectangle, 4½" x 11½" (7 total)

From *each* red print, cut:

- 2 squares, 1⅞" x 1⅞" (14 total); cut squares once diagonally to make 28 triangles
- 1½" square
- 1 template A (7 total)
- 1 template B (7 total)
- 1 rectangle, 5½" x 6½" (7 total)

From *each* green print, cut:

- 1 rectangle, 1½" x 5½" (7 total)

From the floral stripe, cut on the lengthwise grain:

- 4 strips, 5½" x 53½", centering the stripe in the pieces
- 12 strips, 5½" x 11½", centering the stripe in the pieces

Making the Paperwhite Blocks

1. For the Paperwhite blocks, trace the following shapes onto fusible web: two flowerpots, ten leaves, eight stems, and eight flowers, using the patterns on page 61. (See "Fusible Appliqué" on page 153.) Fuse the flowerpots onto red print fabric, the stems and leaves onto green print fabric, and the flowers onto white fabric, and cut them out.

2. Referring to the Paperwhite block diagram for placement, fuse the stems and leaves onto the two 12" background squares. Place the white flowers over the tops of the stems and fuse in place.

3. Fuse the red pots over the bottoms of the stems and leaves. The pot should be about ¼" from the bottom edge of the fabric to allow for trimming. Note that the bottom edges of the flowerpots will be sewn into the seam between the bottom of the block and the sashing.

4. Press the blocks; trim them to 11½" x 11½".

Paperwhite Block

Making the Watering Can Blocks

The Watering Can block is assembled in four vertical segments that are joined together before the top section with the handle is attached to complete the block.

Watering Can Block

1. For the Watering Can blocks, trace seven top handles and seven side handles onto fusible web, using the patterns on page 61. Fuse the handles onto the assorted green print fabrics, and cut them out.

2. Sew the small red and background print triangles together to make four triangle squares.

3. Sew a red-and-background print triangle square to either side of the 1½" red square. Press the seams toward the square.

4. Sew the unit made in step 3 to a 1½" x 4½" background print rectangle. Press the seam toward the rectangle. This is Section 1.

Section 1

5. Sew a red A to a background A, and press the seam toward the red fabric. Sew a 1½" x 2½" background rectangle to this unit along the long background fabric edge.

6. Sew a red B to a background print B. Then sew this unit to the red side of the unit made in step 5.

7. Sew a red-and-background print triangle square from step 2 to a 1½" background square. Sew this unit to the bottom of the unit from step 6 to complete Section 2.

Section 2

8. Sew the 1½" x 5½" green rectangle to the 5½" x 6½" red rectangle to make Section 3.

Section 3

9. Fuse the red side handle to the 3½" x 6½" background rectangle, aligning the two ends of the handle with the raw edges of the rectangle.

10. Sew a red-and-background print triangle square to the end of the remaining 1½" x 2½" background rectangle. Sew this unit

to the bottom of the handle unit from step 9 to complete Section 4.

Section 4

11. Sew segments 1, 2, 3, and 4 together, in order from left to right. Press all seams toward Section 3.

12. Fuse the top handle to the 4½" x 11½" background rectangle to complete Section 5. Sew Section 5 to the top of the unit made in step 11 to complete the block. Repeat to make seven Watering Can blocks.

Assembling the Quilt

1. Referring to the photograph on page 56 for placement, stitch two Watering Can blocks, one Paperwhite block, and four horizontal sashing pieces into a column. Make two of these columns. Press the seams toward the sashing.

2. Stitch the remaining Watering Can blocks into a column, alternating them with four sashing strips.

3. Join the three columns of blocks and four long sashing strips together in alternating vertical rows. Press the seams toward the vertical sashing. To make sure your blocks line up accurately across the rows, you might want to measure and mark your vertical sashing strips to indicate where they should match up with the seam intersections of the block rows.

Quilt Plan

Finishing the Quilt

1. Piece the quilt backing so that it's approximately 6" larger than the quilt top. Layer the quilt top, batting, and backing, and baste, referring to "Layering and Basting" on page 155.

2. Hand or machine quilt as desired. One possibility would be to stipple quilt around each flowerpot and watering can, and then quilt a flower design in the center of each flowerpot or watering can.

3. Trim the excess batting and backing fabric from the quilt. If desired, add a hanging sleeve, referring to page 157 for details.

4. Cut bias strips to make 222" of bias binding and attach it to the quilt, referring to "Binding" on page 157 for details.

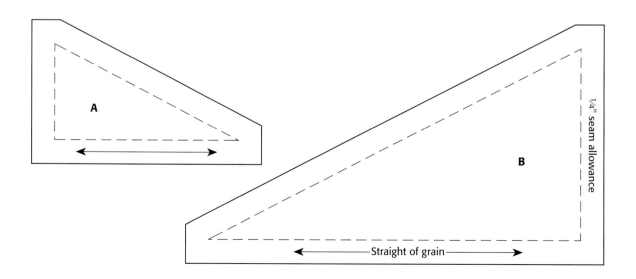

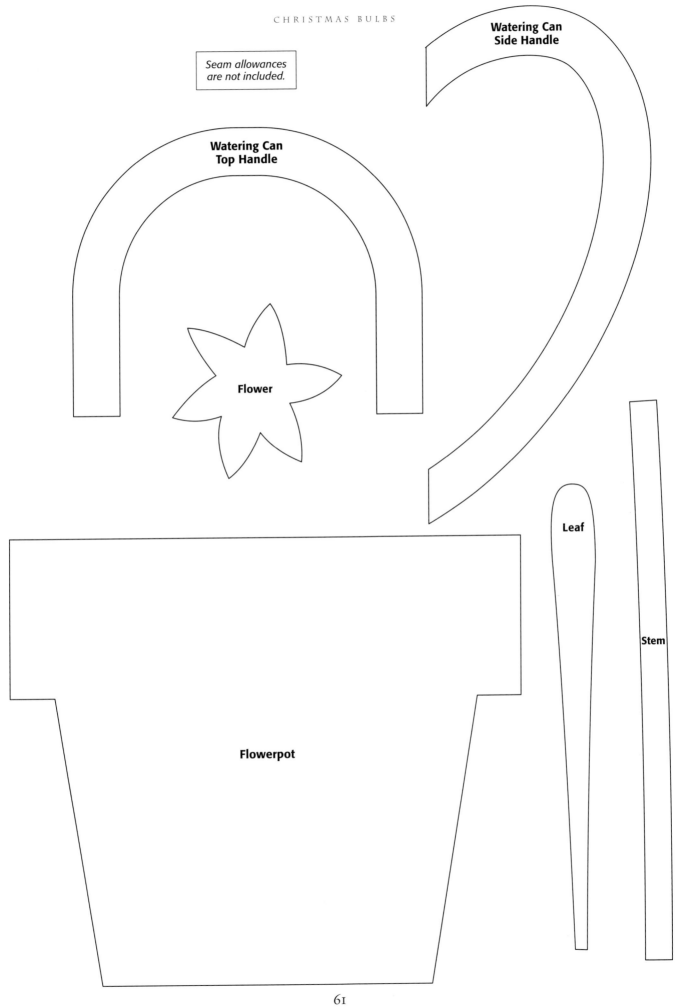

*Seam allowances
are not included.*

**Watering Can
Side Handle**

**Watering Can
Top Handle**

Flower

Leaf

Stem

Flowerpot

CHRISTMAS
INSIDE AND OUT

I love to decorate both indoors and out at Christmastime, so our big, roomy front porch is the perfect place for me to begin. All summer this porch is decorated with white wicker furniture featuring blue checked and striped cushions. To warm up the porch for the holidays, I replace the blue summer accessories with red buffalo-plaid flannel and pillows made from patchwork and Polarfleece. Then I toss in a touch of lace for frosting.

To make outside decorating quick and easy, I stitch pillow covers and slip the summer pillows inside. That way, I don't have to find a place to store extra pillows when the seasons change. If you don't have time during this hectic season to whip up porch accessories, simply tuck lengths of flannel fabric over the summer cushions for an instant seasonal face-lift.

Decorated with my collection of old and new lace tablecloths, red-and-black buffalo-plaid throws, and baskets of greenery, the porch is ready to greet holiday visitors. Sometimes I hang a traditional wreath of greens on our red front door, but for a fun change of pace, a square-shaped red wreath frames a quilt block on the wall adjacent to the door.

The "Home for Christmas" quilt draped over the back of the wicker sofa is one of my favorites. I like it so much that I've made three different versions of it! One stays here on the front porch, and the other two decorate my beach house.

TOP: *Fruits and berries frame a quilt block for an unusual yet festive wreath.*
ABOVE: *Flannel fabric transforms summer cushions and enlivens the decorative pillows.*
For a quick winter makeover, cover summertime pillows with cozy flannel and fleece.
OPPOSITE: *The "Home for Christmas" quilt welcomes guests to the front porch.*

HOME FOR CHRISTMAS

By Nancy J. Martin, Woodinville, Washington, and Cleo Nollette, Seattle, Washington, 2001. Quilted by Frankie Schmitt, Kenmore, Washington.
Finished quilt size: 73½" x 73½"; finished block size: 10".

Welcome family and friends home for the holidays with a warm and cozy house quilt. Tall pine trees—perfect for the season—flank the House blocks. The tree assembly is made easy with a special bias-rectangle technique. Choose a different red for each house or make them all the same. Scrappy or not, this quilt is sure to warm the hearts of all who come to your home for Christmas.

Materials

Yardages are based on 42"-wide fabrics unless otherwise noted.

- 3 yds. light background for blocks and sashing
- 1½ yds. green print for Tall Pine Tree blocks
- 1¼ yds. red print for Tall Pine Tree blocks
- ½ yd. green print for House blocks
- ¼ yd. light red check for House blocks
- ¼ yd. brown print for tree trunks
- 12 fat eighths *or* 1½ yds. total assorted red prints for House blocks
- 1½ yds. green print for border
- 4¼ yds. fabric for backing
- ⅝ yd. red print for bias binding
- 80" x 80" batting

Cutting

Patterns for pieces A–D are on page 71; patterns for pieces E and F are on page 70.

From *each* of the assorted red prints, cut:

- 4 rectangles, 1½" x 4¾" (48 total)
- 2 rectangles, 1½" x 2½" (24 total)
- 2 rectangles, 1½" x 3½" (24 total)
- 1 rectangle, 1½" x 4½" (12 total)
- 2 squares, 2" x 2" (24 total)
- 1 template A (12 total)

From the light red check, cut:

- 1 strip, 3¾" x 42"; cut into 12 rectangles, 2½" x 3¾"
- 1 strip, 2½" x 42"; cut into 24 rectangles, 1½" x 2½"

From the light background, cut:

- 6 sashing strips, 2½" x 62½", on the lengthwise grain
- 2 strips, 1½" x 42"; cut into 12 rectangles, 1½" x 5¾"
- 2 strips, 1½" x 42"; cut into 12 rectangles, 1½" x 5½"
- 2 strips, 2½" x 42"; cut into 24 rectangles, 2" x 2½"
- 1 strip, 3½" x 42"; cut into 12 rectangles, 2" x 3½"
- 12 each of templates C, D, and D reverse*
- 39 each of template F and F reverse*
- 2 strips, 10½ x 42"; cut into 30 sashing strips, 2½" x 10½"

Cut these pieces from the remainder of the width of fabric after cutting the lengthwise sashing strips.

From the green print for House blocks, cut:

✦ 12 template B

From the red print for Tree blocks, cut:

✦ 2 rectangles, 12" x 24"

✦ 5 strips, 2½" x 42"; cut into 26 rectangles, 2½" x 6½"

From the green print for Tree blocks, cut:

✦ 2 rectangles, 12" x 24"

✦ 39 template E

From the brown print, cut:

✦ 13 rectangles, 2½" x 4½"

From the green print for border, cut:

✦ 8 strips, 6" x 42"

Making the House Blocks

The House blocks are assembled in three rows: the house, the roof, and the chimney. The rows are sewn together to complete the block.

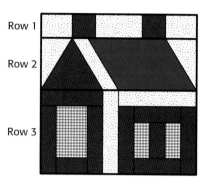

House Block

1. Row 1, the house, is assembled in two parts that are attached with a background strip. To piece the bottom right portion, sew a 1½" x 2½" light red check rectangle to both long edges of a 1½" x 2½" red rectangle. Press the seam allowances toward the red fabric. Then sew a 1½" x 3½" red rectangle to the top and bottom of this unit. Press the seam allowances toward the long red rectangles.

   Sew a 1½" x 4¾" red rectangle to both sides of this unit, and press the seam allowances toward the rectangles you just added. Finally, sew a 1½" x 5½" light background rectangle to the top of the unit.

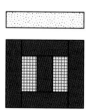

2. To make the bottom left portion, sew a 1½" x 2½" red rectangle to one short end of a 2½" x 3¾" light red check rectangle. Press the seam toward the red fabric. Sew a 1½" x 4¾" red rectangle to each side of this unit and press the seams toward the red fabric. Finally, attach a 1½" x 4½" red rectangle to the top of the unit, and press the seam toward the red fabric.

3. Sew a 1½" x 5¾" light background rectangle between the two sections of the bottom row to connect them. Press the seam allowances toward the darker fabric.

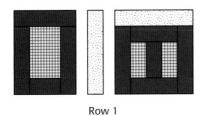

Row 1

4. For Row 2, the roof, sew a light background D triangle to the left side of a red A triangle. Press the seam toward the D piece. Sew a light background C piece to the left side of the green B roof. Sew a D reverse background triangle to the right side of the roof. Press the seam allowances toward the light fabrics. Finally, complete Row 2 by sewing A to C. Press the seam allowance toward the A piece.

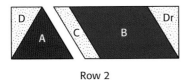

Row 2

5. For Row 3, the chimney row, sew a 2" red square to each short end of a 2" x 3½" light background rectangle. Then sew a 2" x 2½" light background rectangle to the opposite sides of each red chimney. Press all seam allowances toward the red fabric.

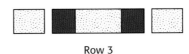

Row 3

6. Sew the three rows together to complete the block, pressing seams away from the center row. Repeat to make 12 House blocks.

Making the Tall Pine Tree Blocks

1. Using the 12" x 24" rectangles of red and green print fabrics for the tree blocks, follow the directions on page 151 to cut and piece 26 bias rectangles and 26 reverse bias rectangles, each measuring 2½" x 4½".

2. Sew the bias rectangles together in pairs, as shown below, paying close attention to the placement of the red and green fabrics. Sew a pair of rectangles to one side of the 2½" x 4½" brown print tree trunk. Sew a reverse pair to the opposite side so that the red fabrics are facing the tree trunk. Press seam allowances toward the brown fabric.

Bias rectangles

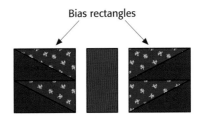

3. Sew the light background F and F reverse triangles to either short side of the green E triangles. Press the seam allowances

toward the background fabric. Sew three triangle units together, pressing the seam allowances toward the long edges of the green triangles.

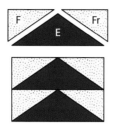

4. Sew a 2½" x 6½" red print for tree blocks rectangle to each side of the stacked triangle unit. Press the seam allowances toward the red fabric.

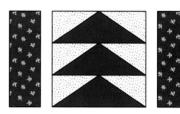

Wicker furniture needn't be stored away during the winter months. New cushion covers and pillows in cheerful, comfy fabrics transform the summer look of the furniture to a winter-holiday welcome for visitors.

5. Sew the green tree top to the trunk unit made in step 2, and press the seam allowance toward the trunk. Repeat to make 13 Tall Pine Tree blocks.

Tall Pine Tree Block
Make 13.

Assembling the Quilt

1. Lay out the blocks and sashing pieces following the quilt assembly diagram below. Row A will have three Tall Pine Tree blocks, two House blocks, and six sashing strips. Make three of Row A. The alternating rows, Row B, will have three House blocks, two Tall Pine Tree blocks, and six sashing strips. Make 2 of Row B.

Row A
Make 3.

Row B
Make 2.

2. Sew the A and B rows together, alternating them and separating them with the 62½" strips of light background sashing. Sew a sashing strip to the top and bottom of the quilt. Press all seam allowances toward the sashing.

Adding the Border

1. Sew the 6" x 42" green print border strips together in pairs. Measure the length of your quilt top through the center and trim two of the long strips to this measurement. Sew the borders to the sides of the quilt, and press the seams toward the borders.

2. Measure the width of your quilt top through the center, including the side borders you just added. Trim the remaining two long strips to this measurement and attach them to the top and bottom of the quilt. Press the seams toward the borders.

Quilt Plan

Finishing the Quilt

1. Piece the quilt backing so that it's approximately 6" larger than the quilt top. Layer the quilt top, batting, and backing, and baste, referring to "Layering and Basting" on page 155.

2. Hand or machine quilt as desired. One possibility would be to outline quilt ¼" inside each seam. You could also quilt a cable pattern in the border.

3. Trim the excess batting and backing fabric from the quilt. If desired, add a hanging sleeve, referring to page 157 for details.

4. Using the red print fabric, cut bias strips to make 304" of bias binding and attach it to the quilt, referring to "Binding" on page 157 for details.

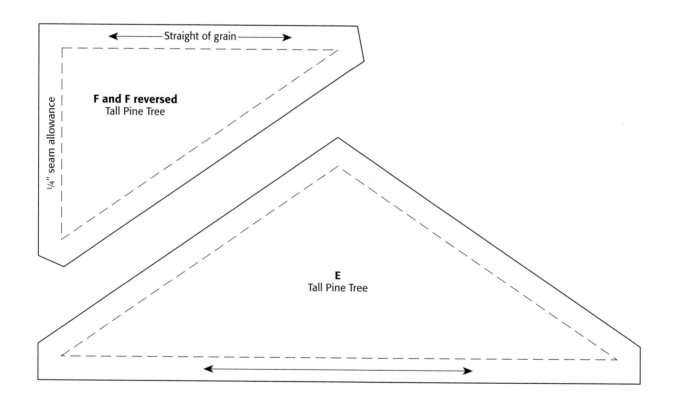

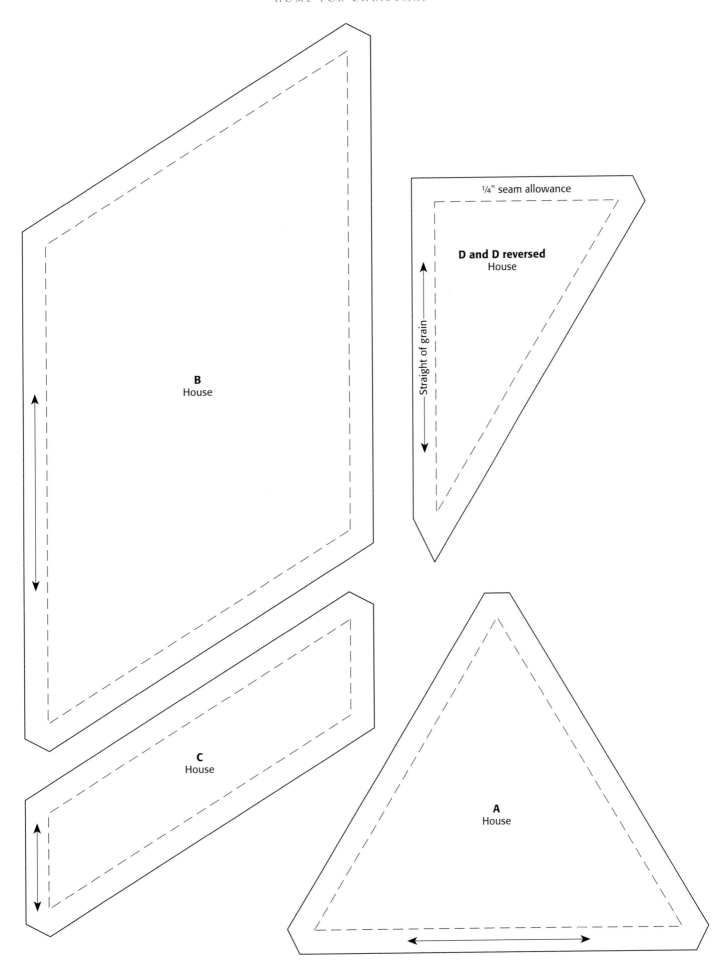

B
House

¼" seam allowance

D and D reversed
House

Straight of grain

C
House

A
House

A CHRISTMAS-SCENTED KITCHEN

I love to spend time in my kitchen, so I take a special delight in decorating this area for the holidays. Here is where all the good scents of the holiday begin, from the baking of Christmas cookies and other treats to the savory aromas of a roasting Christmas dinner. To make some of these seasonal scents linger longer, I like to decorate with fragrant projects that make my kitchen smell good even on days when I'm busy with other holiday tasks—such as decorating or shopping!

A small table near the center island serves as an intimate table for two, making it a perfect spot for a cup of tea and Christmas cookies warm from the oven or a glass of mulled wine or cider.

Culinary herbs grow in pots on the windowsill near jars of preserved lemons, oranges, and cranberries. To round out the scene, I make swags from homegrown rosemary and decorate them with nonedible gingerbread ornaments and miniature kitchen implements. The swags add a festive touch to the window and fill the air with their fragrance.

The red-and-white transferware dishes look even more festive than usual when scented votive candles are placed inside teacups and lit. Combine the candles with the smell of holiday pomanders and rosemary swags, and your kitchen will be filled with wonderful herbal Christmas scents.

ABOVE: *Rosemary swags decorated with small kitchen utensils and gingerbread ornaments flank the windows. Jars of preserved oranges, lemons, and cranberries add a spot of color to the windowsill.*
OPPOSITE: *Raspberry-red kitchen walls dotted with blue dishes serve as a backdrop for holiday decorating touches of fresh greens and berries.*

ROSEMARY SWAG WITH
GINGERBREAD ORNAMENTS

Finished ornament size: approximately 4" tall.

A perfect accent for a Christmassy kitchen, these herbal swags are quite easy to make. If you live in a climate where rosemary grows year-round, you might be able to clip what you need right in your own backyard. If you need to purchase rosemary at the grocery store, you may have to work with shorter lengths. Or you can combine smaller bits of rosemary with an evergreen, such as pine, to extend what you have. You can also use the gingerbread folks to decorate a Christmas tree or as a nice topper for specially wrapped gift boxes.

Materials and Supplies for Swag

Enough for a 6'-long swag

♦ 36 rosemary branches, each approximately 12" long
♦ Floral wire
♦ Wire cutters

Materials and Supplies for Ornaments

Enough for one dozen gingerbread ornaments

♦ 1 cup ground cinnamon (4 oz. can)
♦ 1 tablespoon ground cloves
♦ 1 tablespoon ground nutmeg
♦ ¾ cup applesauce
♦ 2 tablespoons Aleene's Tacky Glue
♦ Krylon Crystal Clear Acrylic Spray
♦ Twelve 6" lengths of fine-gauge wire
♦ Scraps of homespun plaid

CAUTION: *These ornaments are not edible. Keep away from small children, pets, and hungry husbands!*

Making the Swag

1. Lay the rosemary branches in bundles of three branches each. Wire the end of one bundle to the midpoint of a second bundle, tucking the ends of the wire into the greenery to disguise it.

2. Continue wiring new bundles onto the swag until your swag is as long as you want it to be. Repeat to make a second swag in the same manner.

3. Hang a swag on each side of the window, with the needles pointing downward. Hang gingerbread ornaments and small kitchen utensils on each swag.

Making the Gingerbread Ornaments

1. In a medium bowl, combine the cinnamon, cloves, and nutmeg. Stir in the applesauce and glue.

2. Work the mixture with your hands for two to three minutes to form a ball. If the mixture is too dry, add more applesauce; if it's too wet, add more cinnamon. Knead the ball on a cinnamon-sprinkled surface until it holds together well.

3. Divide the dough into four portions for easier handling, and roll out each to ¼" thick. Use a cookie cutter to cut out gingerbread boys and girls.

4. Place the ornaments on cookie sheets. Use a pencil to draw a heart on the gingerbread shape and to make a small hole in each arm for the hanging wire. Make sure the hole goes all the way through the dough.

5. Let the ornaments air-dry. Turn them over from time to time to ensure even drying. Drying will take about four to five days. Place the tray in sunlight for faster results, or dry the ornaments in a warm oven (250° to 300° F) for several hours.

6. When the ornaments are completely dry, paint inside the heart outline and paint two dots for eyes. When the paint is dry, spray the ornaments with acrylic spray.

7. When the acrylic has dried, insert the ends of a 6" piece of wire into the holes in each arm, bending the wire to form a hanging loop. Tie ½" x 4" scraps of plaid homespun to the hanging loops for decoration. To securely hang the ornaments on the swag, use wire ornament hooks and attach them through the hanging loop on the ornament and to the wire on the swag.

Whether in a decorative bowl on their own or mixed in with pomegranates, pine cones, and other large-scale potpourri ingredients, these richly scented pomanders will make your whole house smell good. They're easy to make, but make sure you start early, as they take several weeks to dry.

Materials and Supplies

- 8 oranges, unpeeled
- 3 cups whole cloves
- 2 cups orrisroot powder*
- 1 cup ground cinnamon
- ¾ cup ground allspice
- ½ cup ground nutmeg
- Small cardboard box
- Tissue paper

*Available at your local pharmacy

Directions

1. Lightly draw a design of your choice on the oranges with a pencil. Choose a star, a tree, a stripe, or any other design that is a simple shape.

2. Insert the cloves into the oranges by hand. It will be easier to insert them if you use a large darning needle to poke holes in the orange rind first. Space the cloves about ⅛" apart along the drawn design lines since the oranges will shrink as they dry. You may fill in the center of stars or trees, or simply follow the outline.

3. Blend the orrisroot and spices, and then roll the clove-studded oranges in the spice mixture.

4. Place the oranges in the cardboard box lined with tissue paper. Pour the remaining spice mixture over the oranges, covering the bottom of the box. Cover the box and store it in a warm (not hot), dry place for three to four weeks. Avoid humidity and extreme warmth.

5. When the oranges are thoroughly dry, shake off the excess powder. Your holiday pomanders are now ready to use in a decorative arrangement.

Votive candles set in mismatched teacups illuminate red-and-white transferware dishes and create a warm holiday glow.

GREAT GUEST ROOMS

It's fun to decorate guest rooms for overnight company, making them extra special for the holidays. Small Christmas trees placed in guest rooms lend themselves nicely to being decorated with a theme. Anything can work, from old-fashioned toys to teapots and teacups, angels, or even sewing notions. Finding some unusual items on these small trees is sure to delight your holiday guests.

In the guest room pictured at left, the creamy white walls and white wood trim work quite nicely when the everyday bed linens are replaced with cozy, red plaid sheets and a red-and-white quilt. The "Heart and Home" wall hanging is the focal point of the holiday display of greens, packages, and Santa himself.

A particular challenge I face is that several of my guest rooms have pastel color schemes that don't easily lend themselves to traditional Christmas red and green. In the room shown below, I rely on artificial greens with a tinge of blue in the boughs and small baskets of evergreens with blue and green tones. A wrapped present on a bedside table also adds a welcoming touch.

ABOVE LEFT: *The "Double Nine Patch" quilt hangs on the wall behind a trunk topped with the folded "Cake Stand" quilt and a holiday Santa.*
ABOVE RIGHT: *In another guest bedroom, the "Wonderful World" quilt is part of a blue color scheme. Artificial greenery with blue-green tones helps set the Christmas theme, as does the "Lady of the Lake" quilt draped over the foot of the bed.*
OPPOSITE: *The small "Heart and Home" wall quilt welcomes guests to this colorful bedroom.*

HEART AND HOME

By Nancy J. Martin, Woodinville, Washington, and Cleo Nollette, Seattle, Washington, 2001. Quilted by Martha Hochstetler, Wadema, Minnesota.
Finished quilt size: 33" x 33"; finished block size: 10".

Hanging over the hearth or in a more intimate guest room setting, this holiday house will welcome your guests in style. One simple House block is surrounded by a series of borders that range from basic appliqué to easy-to-piece patchwork, making this a project you'll surely be able to finish in time for Santa's arrival and all the festivities.

Materials

Yardages are based on 42"-wide fabrics unless otherwise noted.

- ✦ 1 yd. white for borders and house background
- ✦ ⅝ yd. dark floral print for border
- ✦ ½ yd. green print for roof and leaves
- ✦ ½ yd. red print for checkerboard
- ✦ ¼ yd. light red print for house, berries, and heart
- ✦ Six 6" squares of assorted red prints
- ✦ 1⅛ yds. fabric for backing
- ✦ ⅜ yd. fabric for bias binding
- ✦ 42" x 42" batting

Cutting

NOTE: *Refer to "Making the House Block" at right for cutting and piecing instructions for the House block; templates A–D are on page 71. Cut and piece this center block before doing the remainder of the cutting below. The appliqué patterns are on page 83.*

From the white fabric, cut:
- ✦ 2 strips, 4½" x 42"; cut strips into 4 border strips, 4½" x 20"
- ✦ 7 squares, 5⅜" x 5⅜"; cut squares twice diagonally to make 28 triangles
- ✦ 6 strips, 2" x 42"

From the red print, cut:
- ✦ 6 strips, 2" x 42"

From the dark floral print, cut:
- ✦ 2 strips, 3" x 24½"
- ✦ 2 strips, 3" x 28¾"

From the assorted red prints, cut:
- ✦ 8 squares, 5⅜" x 5⅜"; cut squares twice diagonally to make 32 triangles

Making the House Block

Referring to "Home for Christmas" on pages 64–67 and the illustration below, cut and piece one House block. Use white fabric for the background, the light red print for the house and chimneys, and the green print for the roof.

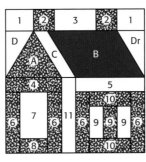

House Block
Make 1.

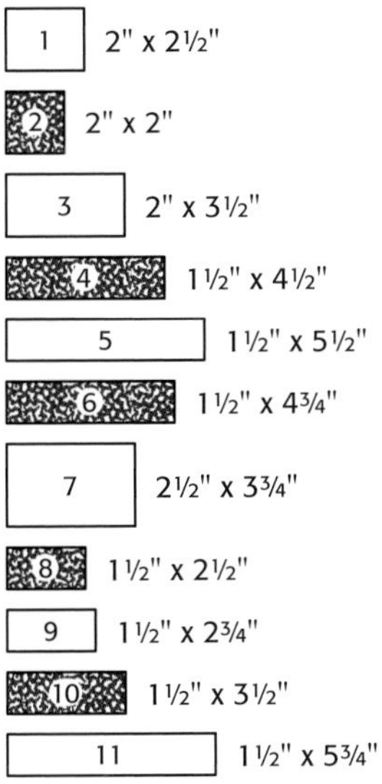

1	2" x 2½"
2	2" x 2"
3	2" x 3½"
4	1½" x 4½"
5	1½" x 5½"
6	1½" x 4¾"
7	2½" x 3¾"
8	1½" x 2½"
9	1½" x 2¾"
10	1½" x 3½"
11	1½" x 5¾"

Adding the Borders

1. Sew the 5" x 20" white strips to each side of the House block, mitering the corners according to the directions on page 154. Press the seams toward the white fabric; then trim the quilt top to 18½" x 18½".

2. Following the directions for fusible appliqué on page 153, cut out and fuse 44 green leaves, 20 light red print berries, and one light red print heart to the quilt top. Use the photograph on page 80 as a placement guide.

3. Stitch the red and white strips together into two strip sets, as shown. Cut the strip sets into 2"-wide segments. You'll need 20 segments.

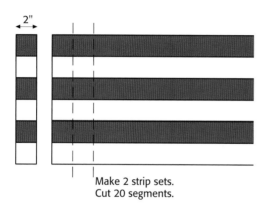

Make 2 strip sets.
Cut 20 segments.

4. Each segment will have six squares in it. For the side borders, sew two segments together end to end, making sure red and white squares alternate along the length of the joined segments. Make four of these joined units. Sew two of the segments together along their long edges so that red squares are opposite white squares, as shown. The borders should be two squares by twelve squares. Repeat to make two side borders.

Side Borders
Make 2.

5. Make the top and bottom borders as you did the side borders, using three segments per border strip instead of two. After each border is assembled, remove a four patch from one end of each border so that each border is two squares by sixteen squares.

Remove
2 segments.

Top and Bottom Borders
Make 2.

6. Stitch the side borders to the quilt top, and press the seam allowances toward the appliqué border. Then sew the top and bottom borders to the quilt top, pressing the seams toward the appliqué border.

7. Sew the 24½" dark print strips to the sides of the quilt, and press the seams toward the dark print fabric. Sew the 28¾" dark print strips to the top and bottom of the quilt, again pressing the seams toward the dark print fabric.

8. For the pieced outer border, join seven white triangles with eight red triangles to make a dogtooth border. Make four of these borders.

9. Stitch a border to each side of the quilt top with the red triangles along the outer edges, as shown. Miter the corners following the directions on page 154.

Quilt Plan

Finishing the Quilt

1. Trim the quilt backing so that it is approximately 4" larger than the quilt top. Layer the quilt top, batting, and backing, and baste, referring to "Layering and Basting" on page 155.

2. Hand or machine quilt as desired. One possibility would be to stitch ¼" away from all leaf and berry edges and ¼" inside each white triangle. Stitch the checkerboard and house in the ditch, and then stitch shingles on the roof. Use a small cable design in the floral border.

3. Trim the excess batting and backing fabric from the quilt. If desired, add a hanging sleeve, referring to page 157 for details.

4. Cut bias strips to make 160" of bias binding and attach it to the quilt, referring to "Binding" on page 157 for details.

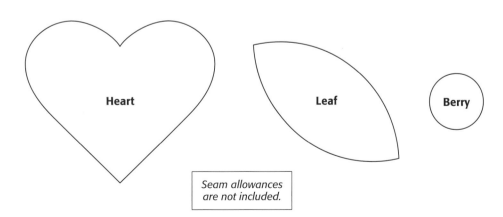

Heart

Leaf

Berry

Seam allowances are not included.

CHRISTMAS AT NANA'S

One of the delights of Christmas is to have a grandchild with whom I can share this special season. My granddaughter, Megan, and I always enjoy our special time together, whether we are baking cookies in the kitchen, crafting ornaments, or telling tales about my childhood Christmases.

To make Megan's visits to our house even more special, I decorate a bedroom so she can have sweet Christmas dreams. In addition to a Santa quilt and pillowcase, a small Christmas tree, toy collections, and other whimsies that children love make going to bed a festive occasion during the holiday season.

TOP: *Don't forget the toys! Stacking Santas and toy soldiers join Santas painted on a bowling ball and pin.*

ABOVE LEFT: *Teddy sports his Christmas hat and scarf.*

ABOVE RIGHT: *A teddy bear tree is the perfect accent in a room decorated for a visiting child.*

OPPOSITE: *The "Santa in the Trees" quilt with its matching pillowcase delights my granddaughter, Megan, when she comes for a holiday sleepover.*

SANTA IN THE TREES QUILT WITH MATCHING PILLOWCASE

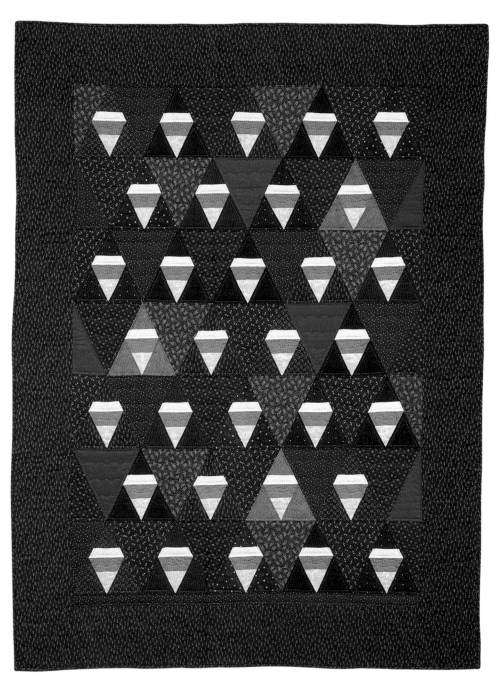

By Nancy J. Martin, Woodinville, Washington, 1991. Quilted by Sue von Jentzen, Granite Falls, Washington.
Finished quilt size: 52½" x 69½".

When my granddaughter, Megan, comes to my house for a holiday sleepover, I put a special quilt and pillowcase on her bed. I call this quilt "Santa in the Trees" because the triangle units can emphasize either the Santas or the Christmas trees, depending on how you place the quilt on the bed. I let Megan decide whether she wants to look at all the Santas or the trees.

Materials

Yardages are based on 42"-wide fabrics.

- 1½ yds. assorted greens for trees and bottom border
- 1¼ yds. red for border
- 1¼ yds. assorted reds for Santas
- ½ yd. off-white for beards
- ⅓ yd. pink print for faces
- ¼ yd. white for fur trim on hat
- 3¾ yds. fabric for backing
- ⅝ yd. fabric for bias binding
- 59" x 76" batting

Additional materials for pillowcase
- ¾ yd. red print for pillowcase
- ¼ yd. contrasting print for facing
- 1¼ yds. narrow piping
- White embroidery floss

Cutting

Patterns for pieces A, B, and C are on page 93.

From the pink print, cut:
- 5 strips, 2" x 42"

From the off-white, cut:
- 5 strips, 3" x 42"

From the white, cut:
- 5 strips, 1½" x 42"

From the assorted red prints, cut:
- 5 strips, 3½" x 42"
- 74 A triangles

From the assorted greens, cut:
- 35 B triangles
- 8 C triangles
- 8 C reverse triangles
- 1 strip, 1½" x 40½"

From the red for border, cut:
- 6 strips, 6½" x 42"

A handcrafted wire Ferris wheel holds an array of small bears.

Piecing the Quilt Top

The Santas for the quilt and pillowcase are strip-pieced. You'll need to make five of each strip set to make enough Santas for both the quilt and the pillowcase. If you don't plan to make the pillowcase, you'll only need to make four of each strip set.

1. Sew the 3" off-white strips and the 2" pink strips together in pairs to make five strip sets, as shown. Make a plastic template of triangle A, and use it to cut 37 Santa face triangles. (Five will be reserved for the pillowcase.) Align the guideline for cutting Santa faces on the pattern with the seam on the strip set for accuracy.

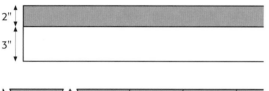
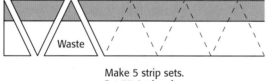

Make 5 strip sets.
Cut 37 A triangles.

2. Sew the 3½" red strips and the 1½"-wide white strips together in pairs to make five strip sets, as shown. Using the A template, cut 37 strip-pieced triangles for Santa hats. Align the lower guideline with the seam on the strip set for accuracy.

Make 5 strip sets.
Cut 37 A triangles.

3. To make a large Santa triangle, sew a red A triangle to each side of the pink-and-white Santa face triangle units. Press the seam allowances toward the red triangles. Then sew the red-and-white Santa hat triangles to the pink sides of the center triangle. Repeat to make 37 Santas—32 for the quilt and 5 for the pillowcase.

4. Stitch five Santas, four green B trees, one green C half-tree, and one green C reverse half-tree into Row A. Repeat to make five of Row A, reserving one of the rows for the pillowcase.

Row A
Make 4.

5. Stitch four Santas, five green B trees, one green C half-tree, and one green C reverse half-tree into Row B. Make three of Row B.

Row B
Make 3.

6. Stitch the rows together, alternating Rows A and B. Remember that you'll have one extra Row A left over for the pillowcase.

Adding the Borders

1. Sew the 1½" x 40½" green strip to the bottom of the quilt top to separate the bottom row of Santas from the red border. Press the seam allowance toward the green border.

2. Sew three of the 6½"-wide red strips together end to end. From this long strip, cut two 6½" x 57½" strips. Sew these strips to the sides of the quilt, and press the seam allowances toward the borders.

3. Sew the remaining three 6½"-wide strips together end to end. From this long strip, cut two 6½" x 52½" strips. Sew these strips to the top and bottom of the quilt, and press the seam allowances toward the borders.

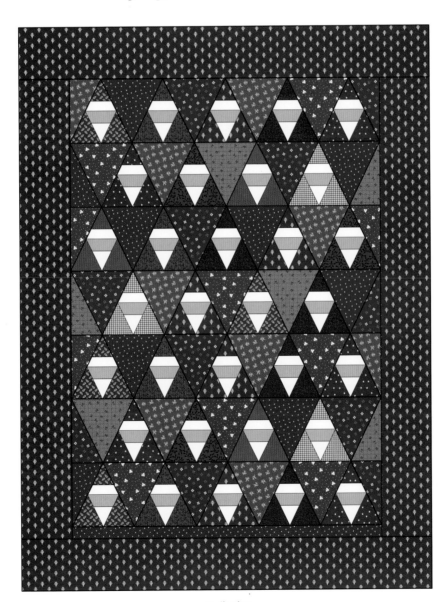

Quilt Plan

Finishing the Quilt

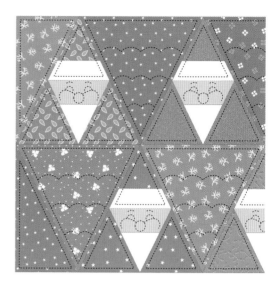

Quilting Suggestion

1. Piece the quilt backing so that it is approximately 6" larger than the quilt top (the yardage allows for the backing to be pieced with a horizontal seam). Layer the quilt top, batting, and backing, and baste, referring to "Layering and Basting" on page 155.

2. Hand or machine quilt as desired. The quilt shown has face details quilted on the pink Santa faces and scalloped lines that suggest tree boughs quilted in the green triangles.

3. Trim the excess batting and backing fabric from the quilt. If desired, add a hanging sleeve, referring to page 157 for details.

4. Cut bias strips to make 254" of bias binding, and attach it to the quilt, referring to "Binding" on page 157 for details.

When this Noah's ark was made, it was called a Sunday toy because it was played with on Sunday—the day of the week when children were allowed to play only with toys having religious themes.

SANTA PILLOWCASE

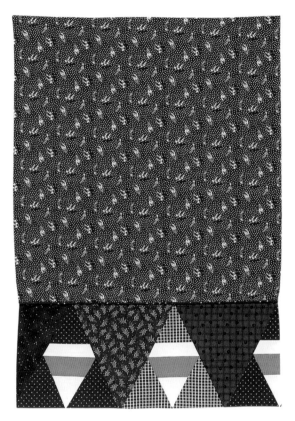

Finished pillowcase size: 20¼" x 29"

Cutting

From the red print, cut:

✦ 1 rectangle, 22" x 42"

Assembling the Pillowcase

1. Using the remaining Row A from "Piecing the Quilt Top" on page 88, embroider the Santa faces using 1 strand of embroidery floss and the quilting design on pattern A, if desired.

2. From the facing fabric, cut a rectangle the same size as the Santa strip (8½" x 40½").

Place the Santa patchwork and facing fabric right sides together, and stitch a ¼" seam along the lower edge of the Santas, as shown. Turn to right side and press the facing.

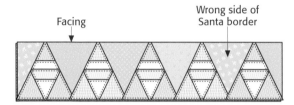

Facing

Wrong side of Santa border

3. Baste the piping to one long edge of the red print rectangle.

4. With right sides together, stitch the top edge of the Santa border to the red print fabric along the basting line of the piping, as shown, being careful not to catch the facing in the seam. Press the seam allowance toward the Santa border.

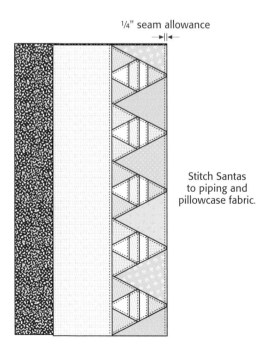

¼" seam allowance

Stitch Santas to piping and pillowcase fabric.

5. Fold under ¼" along the raw edge of the facing fabric and press it in place so that the facing fabric covers the seam allowance. Pin or baste in place.

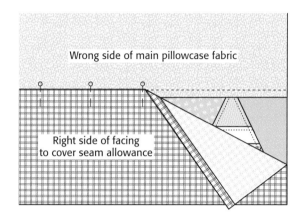

6. On the outside of the pillowcase, topstitch in the ditch along the piping seam to secure the facing in place.

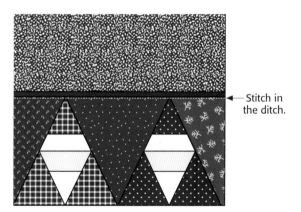

7. Finish the pillowcase with French seams for a neat finish that won't unravel when laundered. Fold the pillowcase in half, *wrong* sides together, matching the seam allowances for the Santa border and piping. Stitch along the top and side edges using a ¼" seam allowance. Turn the pillowcase wrong side out and stitch again using a ½" seam allowance to encase the raw edges of the first seam. Turn pillowcase right side out and press.

TIP

If you have a serger, omit steps 5, 6, and 7 and use the serger to clean-finish the edges on the facing and inside seams.

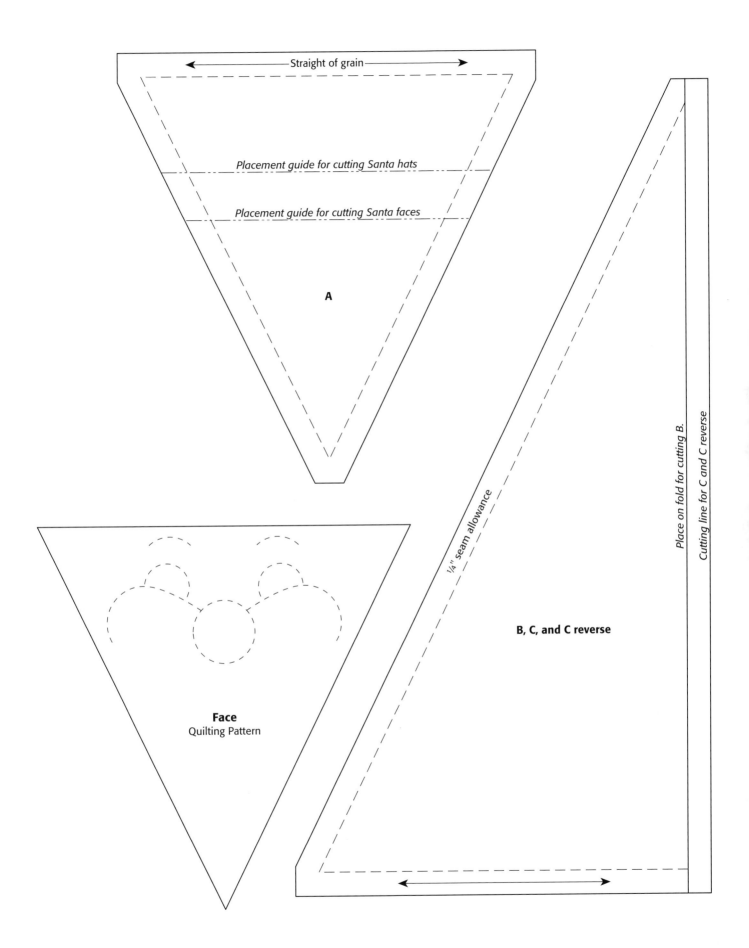

Straight of grain

Placement guide for cutting Santa hats

Placement guide for cutting Santa faces

A

¼" seam allowance

Place on fold for cutting B.

Cutting line for C and C reverse

B, C, and C reverse

Face
Quilting Pattern

CHRISTMAS AT THE BEACH HOUSE

Once Thanksgiving has passed, our family schedules the annual tree-cutting excursion to select the family Christmas trees. We take a flannel quilt along for our festive outdoor picnic. A hot lunch and spiced cider are brought along to warm the hungry tree hunters before we head for home. And we always cut plenty of extra greens to use for decorating and wreath making.

Once the trees make it back to the house, it's time to begin decorating my theme trees. A seafaring theme seems appropriate for this location, so as you enter the beach house, you'll find nautical ornaments on a stairway garland.

The main tree in the living room is decorated with a Pacific Northwest theme, featuring canoes, fishing items, and other outdoor motifs. The "Norway Pine" quilt hangs on the wall behind the tree, a tattered quilt serves as a tree skirt, and two newly made "Burgoyne Surrounded" quilts provide the window dressing.

In the nearby dining area is a tree decked out in a skiing motif (complete with scarf and mittens) and the "Peppermint Pinwheels" quilt. Buffalo-plaid fabric is used to slipcover the dining room chairs and add color to the tabletop topiaries, while the table itself is made festive with "Family Reunion," a table runner made in Christmas fabrics.

Once the decorating at our beach house is complete, there is plenty of time to visit with family and friends. I love to cozy up with a flannel quilt and a plate of cookies in front of a warm fire while the rain splashes outside. The nostalgic "Dick and Jane's Christmas" flannel quilt is perfect to snuggle under while waiting for Santa and the Christmas ships to sail by on Puget Sound.

Holiday topiaries sport a red-and-black buffalo-plaid bow.

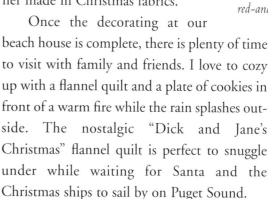

ABOVE: *The stairway garland is adorned with nautical ornaments.*
OPPOSITE: *The "Peppermint Pinwheels" quilt serves as a vibrant backdrop in the rustic dining room of the beach house.*

PEPPERMINT PINWHEELS

By Nancy J. Martin, Woodinville, Washington, 2001. Quilted by Alvina Nelson, Salina, Kansas.
Finished quilt size: 55¾" x 78½"; finished block size: 11⅓".

Reminiscent of peppermint candies tossed in a Christmas stocking, this pinwheel quilt is sure to delight children and adults alike. Big and little pinwheels come together in crisscrossing pathways so full of motion that this quilt seems to twirl. And although the piecing looks complex, the pathways appear once the Starry Path blocks are joined together, making this quilt quite manageable to complete.

Materials

Yardages are based on 42"-wide fabrics unless otherwise noted.

✦ 2½ yds. light background for pinwheels and triangles
✦ 2 yds. green for borders
✦ 1 yd. red for triangles
✦ Six fat quarters assorted greens for pinwheels
✦ 3¼ yds. fabric for backing
✦ ⅝ yd. fabric for bias binding
✦ 62" x 84" batting

Cutting

From the light background, cut:

✦ 36 squares, 7" x 7"
✦ 12 squares, 9¾" x 9¾"; cut squares twice diagonally to make 48 triangles
✦ 12 squares, 4" x 4"; cut squares twice diagonally to make 48 triangles

From the red, cut:

✦ 12 squares, 9¾" x 9¾"; cut squares twice diagonally to make 48 triangles

From the green for borders, cut on the lengthwise grain:

✦ 2 strips, 5½" x 68½"
✦ 2 strips, 5½" x 55¾"

From *each* green print fat quarter, cut:

✦ 6 squares, 7" x 7" (36 total)
✦ 2 squares, 4" x 4" (12 total); cut squares twice diagonally to make 48 triangles

Making Bias Squares

Pair each 7" green square with a 7" light background square, and cut and piece 2½"-wide strips following the directions for bias squares on page 149. Cut a total of 288 bias squares, each 2½" x 2½".

Santas bedecked in buffalo plaid, wooden skis, and woolen mittens decorate our outdoor-themed Christmas tree.

Piecing the Blocks

1. Join six bias squares into a row, as shown, paying careful attention to the color placement. Make 48 of these rows.

Make 48.

2. Join the rows together in pairs, as shown. Notice that you need to rotate one of the rows 180° to make the pattern.

Make 24.

In the beach-house living room, two "Burgoyne Surrounded" quilts serve as curtain panels at each end of the window, while a "Double Nine Patch" quilt top wraps around the rod to serve as a valance.

3. Sew the light background triangles cut from 4" squares to the green triangles cut from 4" squares. Make 48 pairs, as shown. Sew the triangle pairs to the ends of the pinwheel strips made in step 2.

Make 48.

4. Stitch the red triangles cut from 9¾" squares to the background triangles cut from 9¾" squares. Make 48 pairs.

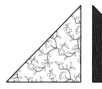

Make 48 pairs.

5. Stitch the triangle units to the pinwheel rows to make 24 blocks.

Make 24.

Assembling the Quilt

1. Alternating the positions of the triangles, stitch four blocks together to make a row. Repeat to make a total of six rows.

Make 6 rows.

2. Alternating the directions of the rows by rotating half of them 180°, stitch them together to assemble the quilt top.

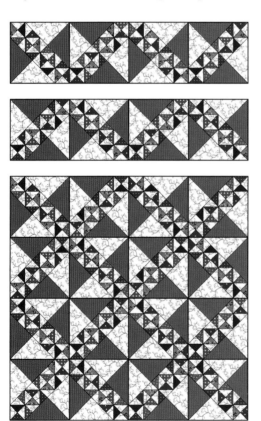

Adding the Borders

1. Stitch the 5½" x 68½" green borders to each side of the quilt top and press the seam allowances toward the borders.

2. Stitch the 5½" x 55¾" green borders to the top and bottom of the quilt top and press the seam allowances toward the borders.

Quilt Plan

Finishing the Quilt

1. Piece the quilt backing so that it's approximately 6" larger than the quilt top. Layer the quilt top, batting, and backing, and baste, referring to "Layering and Basting" on page 155.

2. Hand or machine quilt as desired. The quilt shown has snowflake designs quilted in the small green pinwheels and in the large red pinwheels. (Snowflake quilting patterns are opposite.) Holly leaves and berries are quilted in the borders.

3. Trim the excess batting and backing fabric from the quilt. If desired, add a hanging sleeve, referring to page 157 for details.

4. Cut bias strips to make 277" of bias binding and attach it to the quilt, referring to "Binding" on page 157 for details.

ABOVE: *The main tree in the living room is decorated with a collection of Northwest-themed ornaments. The "Norway Pine" quilt hangs on the wall behind the tree.*
RIGHT: *The master bedroom showcases a vintage quilt and patriotic pillows. For the holiday season, a red-and-green "House" quilt is displayed on the wall and a small tree decked with Americana ornaments perches on a corner table.*

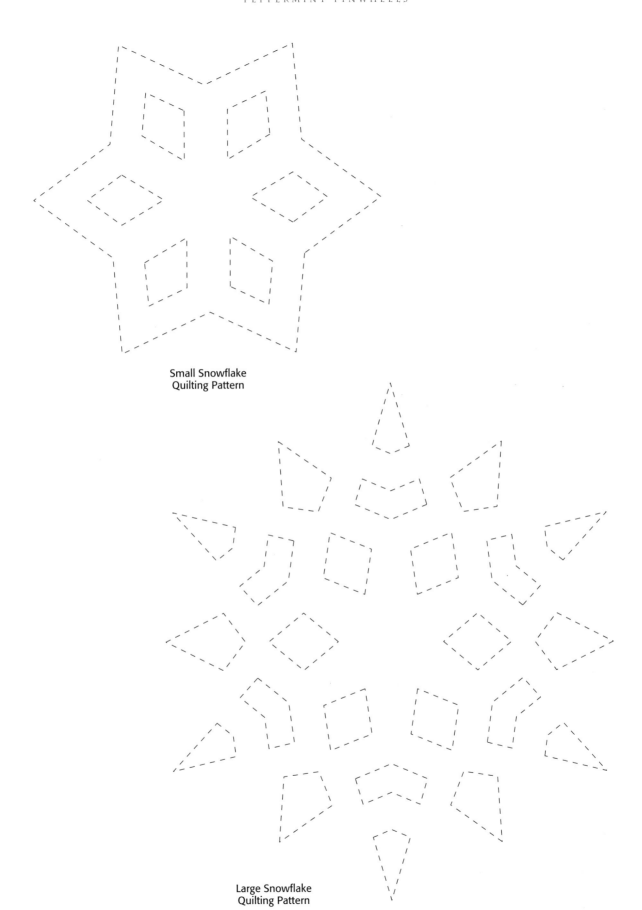

Small Snowflake
Quilting Pattern

Large Snowflake
Quilting Pattern

DICK AND JANE'S
CHRISTMAS FLANNEL QUILT

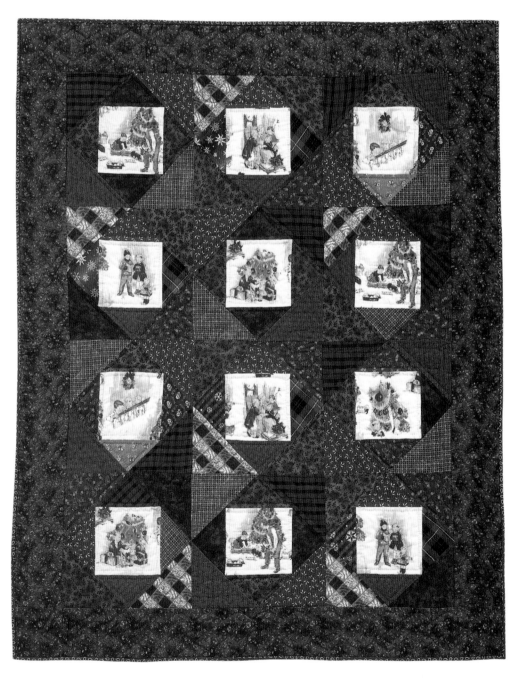

By Nancy J. Martin, Woodinville, Washington, 2001. Quilted by Mattie Mast and Mary Mast, Fredericksburg, Ohio.
Finished quilt size: 45" x 57"; finished block size: 12".

Whether or not you grew up with the Dick and Jane series of readers, you'll love this endearing flannel Christmas fabric. Of course, you can choose any novelty print fabric to use as the center of your quilt blocks, be it polar bears, angels, or Christmas trees. Choose a fun theme-print fabric and base your quilt around that.

Materials

Yardages are based on 42"-wide fabrics unless otherwise noted. Because flannel fabrics are prone to shrinking, we've allowed extra fabric so that you won't run short after prewashing your fabrics.

- 1⅔ yds. green flannel for border
- 1 fat quarter *each* of six cranberry print flannels
- 1 fat quarter *each* of six green print flannels
- ¾ yd. novelty print flannel
- 2¾ yds. flannel for backing
- ½ yd. cotton or flannel for bias binding
- 51" x 63" batting

Cutting

From the novelty print, cut:
- 12 squares, 6½" x 6½", centering the novelty print within the square (see page 153 for information on cutting motif fabric)

From *each* cranberry fat quarter, cut:
- 2 squares, 5⅛" x 5⅛" (12 total); cut squares once diagonally to make 24 triangles
- 2 squares, 6⅞" x 6⅞" (12 total); cut squares once diagonally to make 24 triangles

From *each* green fat quarter, cut:
- 2 squares, 5⅛" x 5⅛" (12 total); cut squares once diagonally to make 24 triangles
- 2 squares, 6⅞" x 6⅞" (12 total); cut squares once diagonally to make 24 triangles

From the green for border, cut on the lengthwise grain:
- 2 strips, 4¾" x 48½"
- 2 strips, 4¾" x 45"

Piecing the Blocks

1. Sew two small green triangles to opposite sides of a novelty print square. Press the seams toward the square. Sew two more small green triangles to the remaining two sides of the square, and press the seam allowances toward the square.

Snuggled under the cozy flannel "Dick and Jane's Christmas" quilt in front of a warm fire is a wonderful way to await the arrival of the Christmas ships on Puget Sound.

2. Sew two large cranberry triangles to opposite sides of the block made in step 1, pressing seam allowances toward the center of the block. Repeat, sewing two more large cranberry triangles to the remaining two sides of the block. Press seam allowances toward the center of the block. Repeat to make six blocks with cranberry triangles on the outside.

Make 6.

3. To make the alternate blocks with green triangles on the outside, repeat steps 1 and 2, sewing the small cranberry triangles to the novelty print squares first. Then sew the large green triangles to the outsides of the blocks. Repeat to make six of these blocks.

Make 6.

Assembling the Quilt

1. Arrange the blocks into four rows of three blocks each, alternating the cranberry and green blocks.

2. Sew the blocks together into rows, and then join the rows.

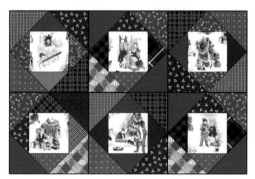

ABOVE: *Folk art Santas gather in front of a collection of brown transferware.*
BELOW: *Hand-knit stockings hang from a fireplace mantel, while rustic Santas rest amid a collection of miniature chairs and brown transferware dishes.*

Adding the Borders

1. Sew the 4¾" x 48½" strips to the sides of the quilt top. Press the seam allowances toward the borders.

2. Sew the 4¾" x 45" strips to the top and bottom of the quilt top. Press the seam allowances toward the borders.

Finishing the Quilt

1. Piece the quilt backing so that it's approximately 6" larger than the quilt top. Layer the quilt top, batting, and backing, and baste, referring to "Layering and Basting" on page 155.

2. Hand or machine quilt as desired. One possibility would be to quilt ½" inside each triangle block, except for the six places where the four large triangles come together. A snowflake or poinsettia quilting design would be nice in these areas.

Hand quilting with pearl cotton is another good option for flannel quilts. Taking big stitches with this chunky thread lets you finishing the quilting quickly, and the thread shows up well in the nap of the fabric.

3. Trim the excess batting and backing fabric from the quilt. If desired, add a hanging sleeve, referring to page 157 for details.

4. Cut bias strips to make 214" of bias binding and attach it to the quilt, referring to "Binding" on page 157 for details.

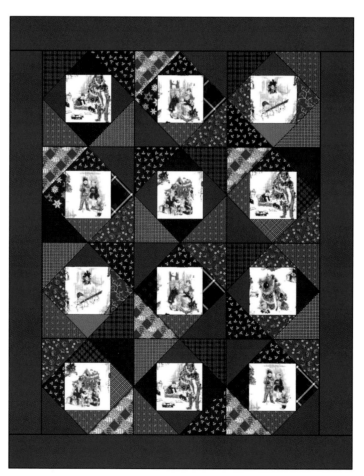

Quilt Plan

PART TWO

CHRISTMAS

WITH FRIENDS

CHRISTMAS WITH CLEO

Cleo Nollette loves red. She dresses in red, collects red-and-white transferware dishes, adores red fabrics and red quilts, and even has a great red bedroom. One of her bedrooms is decorated in a red toile fabric that I designed several years ago. Recently, many great toile fabrics have become available, much to our delight. Cleo's house, with its red roof and red accents, always looks festive, but especially so at Christmas.

As the oldest of thirteen siblings, Cleo is an aunt to many nieces and nephews, as well as having many young friends who think of her as an auntie. In the special bedroom shown here, you'll often find a niece visiting for a few days, snuggled under the "One Star" quilt. It's a wonderful quilt to make for the holidays, and the easy design stitches up quickly, which is particularly beneficial for all those last-minute quiltmakers!

It's fun to visit Cleo's house and enjoy the myriad projects she is always working on. In addition to her own projects, she finds time to come and stitch with me in my home. Cleo has worked with me since 1992. Her calling card says assistant to the president, a position with a varied job description. You might find her helping me stitch quilts for publication, shopping for props for photo shoots, or helping to cook a gourmet luncheon for forty people. She is a true friend who is available to help me out

in a pinch, and she always does so with grace and humor.

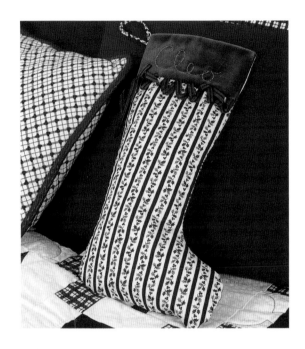

TOP AND ABOVE: *A cheery Christmas stocking coordinates with a variety of red pillows and the "Homecoming Wreath" quilt.*
OPPOSITE: *"One Star" covers the bed beneath the "Cake Stand" wall quilt. The small "Homecoming Wreath" quilt rests on the pillows.*

ONE STAR

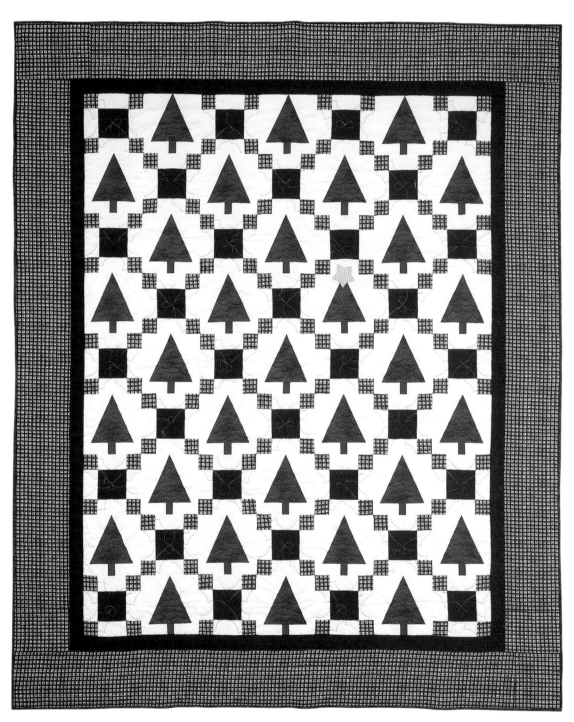

By Cleo Nollette, Seattle, Washington, 2001. Quilted by Dawn Kelly, Slagle, Idaho.
Finished quilt size: 75½″ x 91½″; finished block size: 8″.

Puss in the Corner blocks, which are quite easy to piece, alternate with Tree blocks to make a bright and cheery Christmas bed quilt. I chose a whimsical, wavy plaid to add to the fun, and a single star shines atop one of the trees. Holly leaf quilting in the red-and-white blocks completes the holiday theme with a flourish. Snuggled under this quilt, who could help but dream of sugarplum fairies?

—CLEO NOLLETTE

Materials

Yardages are based on 42"-wide fabrics unless otherwise noted.

- 2¾ yds. white print for background
- 2½ yds. red plaid for blocks and border
- 1⅛ yds. red print for blocks and border
- 1 yd. green print for Tree blocks
- ⅛ yd. brown or green print for tree trunks
- 4" scrap of gold for star
- 5¼ yds. fabric for backing
- ½ yd. green print for binding
- 82" x 98" batting

Cutting

From the white print, cut:
- 4 strips, 4½" x 42"
- 8 strips, 2½" x 42"
- 4 strips, 4" x 42"
- 5 strips, 7" x 42"

From the red plaid, cut:
- 8 strips, 2½" x 42"
- 8 strips, 8" x 42"

From the red print, cut:
- 4 strips, 4½" x 42"
- 7 strips, 2½" x 42"

From the green print, cut:
- 4 strips, 7" x 42"

From the brown or green print, cut:
- 2 strips, 1½" x 42"

Piecing the Puss in the Corner Blocks

1. Sew a 2½"-wide red plaid strip on either side of 4½"-wide white print strip. Press the seam allowances toward the plaid fabric. Repeat to make a total of four strip sets. Cut the strip sets into sixty-four 2½"-wide segments.

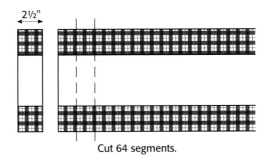

Cut 64 segments.

2. Sew a 2½"-wide white print strip on either side of a 4½"-wide red print strip. Press the seam allowances toward the red fabric. Repeat to make a total of four strip sets. Cut the strip sets into thirty-two 4½"-wide segments.

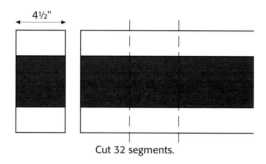

Cut 32 segments.

3. Sew 2½"-wide segments to the tops and bottoms of the 4½"-wide segments to complete 32 Puss in the Corner blocks.

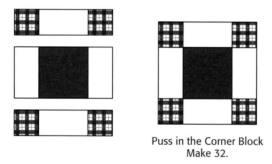

Puss in the Corner Block
Make 32.

Piecing the Tree Blocks

1. Sew a 4"-wide white print strip to either side of a 1½"-wide brown or green strip. Repeat to make a second strip set. Press the seam allowances toward the brown or green fabric. Cut the strip sets into thirty-one 2" segments.

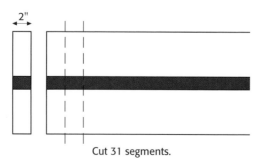

Cut 31 segments.

2. Make a plastic template from the A pattern on page 117. Use it to cut 31 triangles from the 7"-wide green print strips.

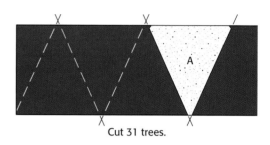

Cut 31 trees.

3. Make a plastic template from the B and B reversed pattern on page 117. With the 7"-wide white background strips folded in half, use the template to cut 31 B and 31 B reverse pieces. (When you cut the B pieces on folded fabric, you'll automatically be cutting a B reverse piece.)

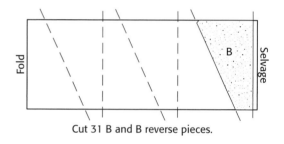

Cut 31 B and B reverse pieces.

4. Sew a B and a B reverse piece to the two long edges of a green triangle. Repeat for all 31 triangles. Press the seam allowances toward the green fabric.

5. Sew the 2"-wide segments from step 1 to the bottom of each green triangle unit to complete 31 Tree blocks. Press the seam allowances toward the green triangles.

Tree Block
Make 31.

Assembling the Quilt

1. Stitch the blocks together in rows, alternating the Puss in the Corner and Tree blocks. Make five rows that start and end with Puss in the Corner blocks and four rows that start and end with Tree blocks.

2. Stitch the rows together, alternating the placement of your rows.

3. Using the pattern on page 116 and the appliqué method of your choice, cut out one gold star and appliqué it to the Tree block of your choice.

Adding the Borders

1. Stitch together two of the 2½"-wide red print strips end to end. Measure the length of your quilt top through the center, and trim the border to this length. Sew two more of the 2½"-wide red strips together and cut them to this length as well. Sew the borders to the sides of your quilt top. Press the seam allowances toward the red borders.

2. Stitch the remaining three red print strips together end to end. Measure the width of the quilt top through the center, including the side borders you just added. From the long red print strip, cut two borders to this length. Sew the borders to the top and bottom of the quilt, and press the seam allowances toward the red borders.

3. Sew the 8"-wide red plaid strips together, end to end, in pairs. Measure the length of your quilt top through the center, and trim two of the border strips to this length. Sew the borders to the sides of the quilt. Press the seam allowances toward the red plaid fabric.

4. Measure the width of your quilt top through the center, and trim the remaining two border strips to this measurement. Sew the borders to the top and bottom of the quilt, and press the seam allowances toward the red plaid borders.

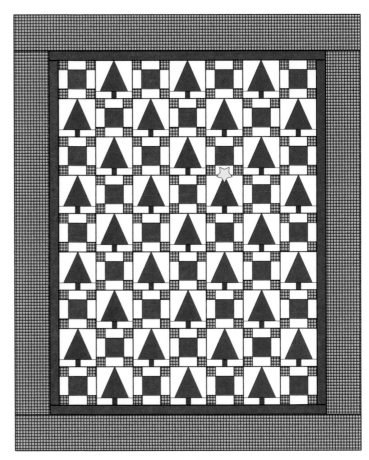

Quilt Plan

Finishing the Quilt

1. Piece the quilt backing so that it's approximately 6" larger than the quilt top. Layer the quilt top, batting, and backing, and baste, referring to "Layering and Basting" on page 155.

2. Hand or machine quilt as desired. The quilt shown is machine quilted with red, white, and green variegated thread in a holly leaf pattern that connects from one Puss in the Corner block to another. The Tree blocks are quilted with scalloped lines that suggest tree boughs. The plaid border is quilted with straight lines, following the printed plaid lines as guidelines.

3. Trim the excess batting and backing fabric from the quilt. If desired, add a hanging sleeve, referring to page 157 for details.

4. Using the green print for binding, cut nine binding strips to make and attach straight-grain binding, referring to "Binding" on page 157 for details.

Star
*Seam allowance
is not included.*

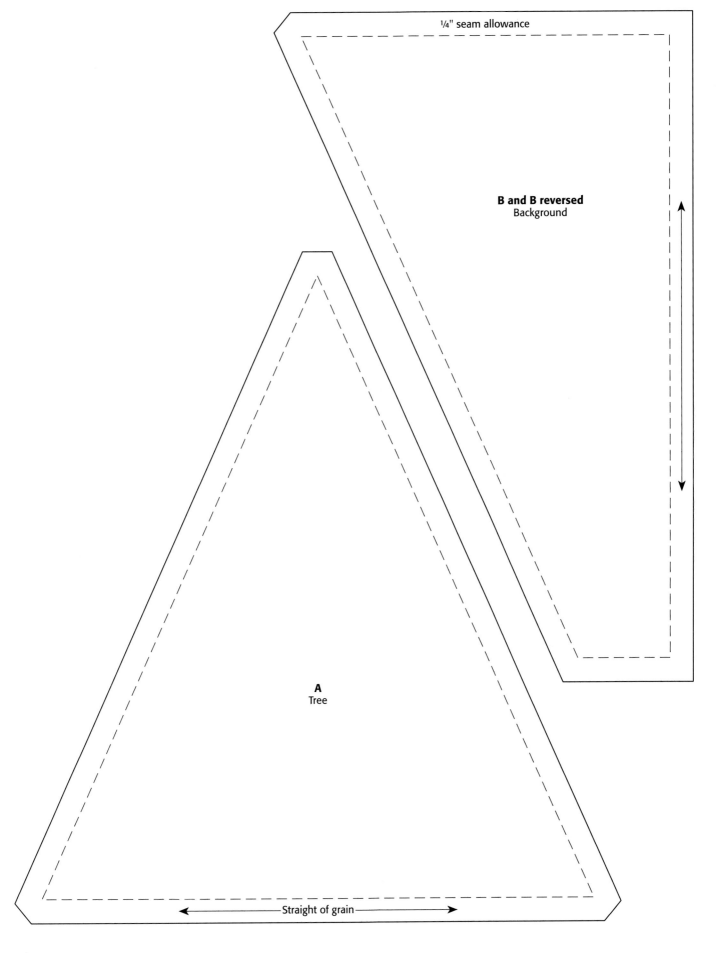

¼" seam allowance

B and B reversed
Background

A
Tree

Straight of grain

A LITTLE QUILTS CHRISTMAS

I can always count on my friends from Little Quilts to come up with creative decorating ideas for the holidays. Although they live in Marietta, Georgia, miles away from Seattle, our twice-yearly visits at Quilt Market enable us to update each other on new houses, new color schemes, and new decorating ideas.

Alice Berg, Sylvia Johnson, and Mary Ellen Von Holt were among the first to use quilts in their home decor—and not just on the bed. They began publishing patterns for their Little Quilts company in 1984. Their little quilts were displayed on walls, tables, and chairs all through the house. In fact, their first book is aptly named *Little Quilts all through the House*. This book is still one of the bestselling titles for Martingale & Company. Three subsequent books followed: *Celebrate with Little Quilts, Living with Little Quilts,* and *Bunnies by the Bay Meets Little Quilts*.

Alice's big red saltbox colonial home often served as the backdrop for Little Quilts photo shoots. The three women arrange small quilts, bears, and hooked rugs in a pleasing setting, often in front of the fireplace. The "Santa's on His Way" quilt on the wall in the photo opposite makes a great Christmas project for young and old.

The key to the Little Quilts decorating style is summed up in three tips. First, look for items of the same color or theme to add to a collection. For example, add doll clothes, tea sets, valentines, and toys to a display of old dolls. Second, begin by arranging the larger quilts and pieces, then fill in with the smaller ones. Third, arrange things in a whimsical way, as if someone had been there playing and just walked away.

ABOVE: *A variety of red-and-white quilts grouped with doll furniture and other toys makes a whimsical display.*
OPPOSITE: *Antique quilts, both large and small, decorate this inviting fireside seating area.*
The "Santa's on His Way" wall quilt adds a spot of holiday charm.

SANTA'S ON HIS WAY

By Little Quilts, Marietta, Georgia, 1996.
Finished quilt size: 19" x 25"; finished block size: 5".

Here comes Santa, and he's marching right across your quilt! We made this project in the typical Little Quilts style—it's quick and easy, and perfect for a last-minute decorating accent or gift. Whether you hang this quilt on a wall, tuck it in a basket with greens and pinecones, or display it on a doll bed, these delightful little fellows will bring a holiday chuckle to all who see them.

—LITTLE QUILTS

Materials

Yardages are based on 42"-wide fabrics unless otherwise noted.

+ ⅔ yd. tan print for border
+ Six scraps of assorted tan fabrics, at least 6" square, for backgrounds
+ Assorted red, green, gold, blue, and black print scraps for Santas, trees, and sashing
+ Scrap of muslin for Santa beards
+ ⅔ yd. fabric for backing
+ ¼ yd. red print for binding
+ 22" x 28" batting
+ ½ yd. lightweight fusible web
+ Six ⅜" white buttons
+ Black and off-white embroidery floss or pearl cotton

Cutting

From assorted tan backgrounds, cut:

+ 6 squares, 5½" x 5½"

From assorted green, gold, blue, and black prints, cut:

+ 17 rectangles, 1½" x 5½"

From a red print scrap, cut:

+ 12 squares, 1½" x 1½"

From the tan print for border, cut:

+ 2 strips, 3¼" x 42"; subcut into 2 strips, 3¼" x 19½", and 2 strips, 3¼" x 19"

Appliquéing the Blocks

1. Trace four Santas (bodies, faces, beards, hats, arms, hands, and feet) onto fusible web, using the patterns on page 125 and allowing at least ¼" between the traced shapes. Also trace two trees and two tree trunks (see page 125) onto fusible web. Following the manufacturer's directions, cut out the fusible shapes and fuse them onto the wrong side of the appropriate color fabrics. Cut out the shapes along the drawn lines.

2. Following the block diagram below, arrange the appliqué shapes on the tan background squares in this order: First, lay the Santa suit in place. Then, tuck the feet under the legs and place the arm on the suit. Tuck the hand under the arm, tuck the face and suit under the beard, and put the hat over the beard and face. Fuse in place. Repeat to make four Santa blocks.

Santa Block
Make 4.

3. Following the block diagram below, center the trees in the remaining two tan squares and tuck the tree trunks under the trees. Fuse in place. Repeat to make two Tree blocks.

Tree Block
Make 4.

4. To securely hold the fused appliqués in place, blanket stitch around the shapes. In the quilt shown, the shapes were stitched by hand using black embroidery floss, except for the beards, which were stitched with off-white floss. If you prefer, you can use pearl cotton or even do the blanket stitching by machine. Add a French knot "eye" to each Santa face using black floss.

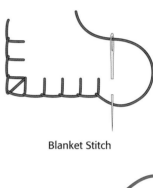

Blanket Stitch

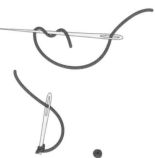

French Knot

Assembling the Quilt

1. Following the diagram at right, lay out the Santa and Tree blocks in three rows. The Santa and Tree block rows have two blocks each and three sashing strips. The sashing rows have two sashing strips and three red print sashing squares each. Sew the pieces together to form the rows. Press all seams toward the sashing strips.

2. Sew the rows together, pressing the seam allowances toward the sashing rows.

This sampler quilt belongs to Mary Ellen Von Holt, who was given the Christmas-theme blocks by her quiltmaking friends. It creates a warm setting for the quilts and holiday items on the benches below it.

Adding the Border

1. Sew the 3¼" x 19½" tan border strips to the sides of the quilt. Press the seam allowances toward the borders.

2. Sew the 3¼" x 19" tan border strips to the top and bottom of the quilt. Press the seam allowances toward the borders.

Finishing the Quilt

1. Trim the quilt backing so that it is approximately 4" larger than the quilt top. Layer the quilt top, batting, and backing, and baste, referring to "Layering and Basting" on page 155.

2. Hand or machine quilt as desired. The quilt shown is quilted in the ditch around each block and around the Santas and the trees. The sashing and sashing squares are quilted with Xs. The border features quilted stars that are connected with swirling lines. As a final detail, buttons are sewn to the tip of each Santa hat and tree top with black embroidery floss.

3. Trim the excess batting and backing fabric from the quilt. If desired, add a hanging sleeve, referring to page 157 for details.

4. Make and attach straight-grain binding, referring to "Binding" on page 157 for details.

Quilt Plan

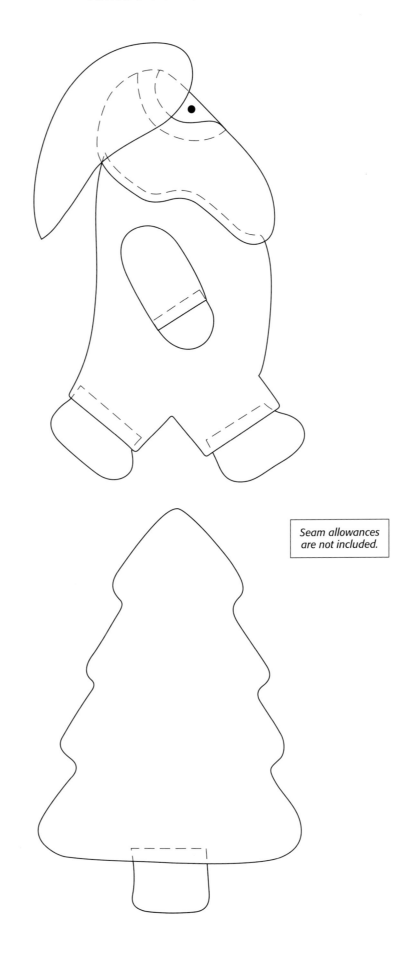

Seam allowances
are not included.

A FLANNEL CHRISTMAS

Sandy Bonsib shares so much of herself with others that it's just a delight to spend time with her. One of the most popular quilting teachers in the Seattle area, she has taught at In The Beginning Fabrics since 1993. Her first classes were based on her wonderful folk art quilts, which led to her first book, *Folk Art Quilts.*

From there, Sandy explored photo transfer quilts and along with her business partner, Lynn Ahlers, developed a very successful photo transfer paper. Her two books featuring photo transfer quilts, *Quilting Your Memories* and *Quilting More Memories,* have inspired many people to create quilts that preserve family memories. Sandy rarely visits the Martingale office without a huge plate of homemade chocolate chip cookies to share, and she has even immortalized the recipe on one of her photo transfer quilts.

Flannel quilts are another favorite of Sandy's, and this love led to her fourth book, *Flannel Quilts,* in 2001. She has taught countless students how to design and stitch using flannel, so it is not surprising that her Christmas quilt is made from flannel. It hangs in the living room of her Cougar Mountain home in Issaquah, Washington.

The Bonsib house abounds with animals, and Sandy is usually accompanied by a guide-dog puppy that she is training. She grows to love them and is sad when they leave for more advanced training at Guide Dogs for the Blind, but Sandy is quite dedicated to her important job as each pup's first trainer.

ABOVE LEFT: *Folk art decorates the mantel.*
ABOVE RIGHT: *Folded over the back of the rocker is a quilt named "Color Me Bright."*
OPPOSITE: *In the soothing glow of Sandy Bonsib's living room, "All Hearts Are Home for Christmas" takes center stage next to the wall quilt "My Favorite Things."*

ALL HEARTS ARE
HOME FOR CHRISTMAS

By Sandy Bonsib, Issaquah, Washington, 2001. Quilted by Becky Kraus, Bellevue, Washington.
Finished quilt size: 80¼" x 98¾"; finished block size: 18½" x 18½".

I love working with flannel fabrics, and I couldn't imagine anything more cozy to use for a Christmas quilt. The soft feel of the fabric together with the folksy style of the piecing and appliqué are the perfect complement to our log cabin home. With so many fabulous flannels available today, you can choose flannels in patterns and colors to suit any decor. But watch out: Once you top your bed in a snuggly flannel quilt, you won't want to get out of bed!

—SANDY BONSIB

Materials

Yardages are based on 42"-wide fabrics.

- ✦ 3 yds. Christmas print flannel for outer border
- ✦ 1¾ yds. red plaid flannel for Heart blocks
- ✦ 1 yd. *each* of five gold flannels for Rail Fence blocks
- ✦ 1 yd. green flannel for middle border
- ✦ ⅔ yd. red flannel for inner border
- ✦ ½ yd. gold flannel for hearts
- ✦ 6 yds. fabric for backing
- ✦ ¾ yd. fabric for binding

Cutting

The heart pattern is on page 133.

From *each* gold for blocks, cut:
- ✦ 8 strips, 2¾" x 42" (40 strips total)

From the gold for hearts, cut:
- ✦ 12 hearts

From the red plaid, cut:
- ✦ 12 squares, 12" x 12"

From the red for inner border, cut:
- ✦ 7 strips, 2" x 42"

From the green, cut:
- ✦ 8 strips, 2⅝" x 42"

From the Christmas print, cut on the lengthwise grain:
- ✦ 2 strips, 9" x 82"
- ✦ 2 strips, 9" x 80½"

From the binding fabric, cut:
- ✦ 10 strips, 2" x 42"

Making the Blocks

1. Piece five different gold strips together. Press all the seams in the same direction. Repeat to make eight strip sets. Cut the strip sets into twenty-four 11¾" segments.

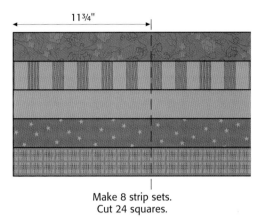

11¾"

Make 8 strip sets.
Cut 24 squares.

2. Cut all the Rail Fence units in half diagonally to create 48 triangles. Be sure to cut all blocks in the same direction.

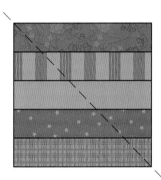

3. Using your favorite appliqué method, appliqué a heart on-point in each 12" red plaid square. After the appliqué is complete, trim the blocks to 11¾", making sure that the heart is centered in the red plaid square.

4. Sew the Rail Fence triangles to opposite sides of each Heart block. Press the seam allowances toward the triangles. Trim the triangle tips even with the edges of the Heart block, as shown.

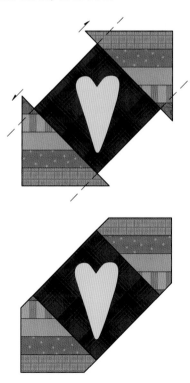

5. Sew Rail Fence triangles to the remaining sides of each Heart block. Press the seam allowances toward the triangles. Trim all the blocks to 19" x 19", making sure the red plaid square is centered in the block as you trim it.

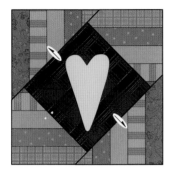

Make 12.

Assembling the Quilt

1. Sew the blocks together in four horizontal rows of three blocks each. Press the seam allowances in opposite directions from row to row.

2. Join the rows and press the seam allowances all in one direction.

Adding the Borders

1. Join six of the 2"-wide red strips end to end into three pairs. From two of these long strips, cut two pieces 74½" long. Sew these strips to the sides of the quilt top, pressing the seam allowances toward the red strips. Sew the remaining 2"-wide red strip to the remaining pair of strips. From this long strip, cut two pieces 59" long. Sew these strips to the top and bottom of the quilt top, pressing the seam allowances toward the red strips.

This woolly Santa has found a fitting spot on the hearth in front of Sandy's flannel quilt.

2. Join the 2⅝"-wide green strips end to end in pairs. From these long strips, cut two pieces 77½" long. Sew these strips to the sides of the quilt top, pressing the seam allowances toward the green strips. From the remaining strips, cut two pieces 63¼" long. Sew these strips to the top and bottom of the quilt top, pressing the seam allowances toward the green strips.

3. Sew the 81¾"-long Christmas print border strips to the sides of the quilt top. Press the seam allowances toward the outer border. Sew the 80¼"-long Christmas print border strips to the top and bottom of the quilt top. Press the seam allowances toward the outer border.

Finishing the Quilt

1. Piece the quilt backing and trim it so that it is approximately 6" larger than the quilt top. Layer the quilt top, batting, and backing, and baste, referring to "Layering and Basting" on page 155.

2. Hand or machine quilt as desired. The quilt shown is machine quilted. The appliquéd gold hearts are surrounded by echo quilting in the red plaid background squares, while the Rail Fence parts of the blocks are quilted in a feather pattern. A twisting vine pattern fills the green middle border, and large meandering is used in the Christmas print border—a good choice, since the print is too busy to show off an intricate quilting design.

3. Trim the excess batting and backing fabric from the quilt. If desired, add a hanging sleeve, referring to page 157 for details.

4. Make and attach straight-grain binding, referring to "Binding" on page 157 for details.

Quilt Plan

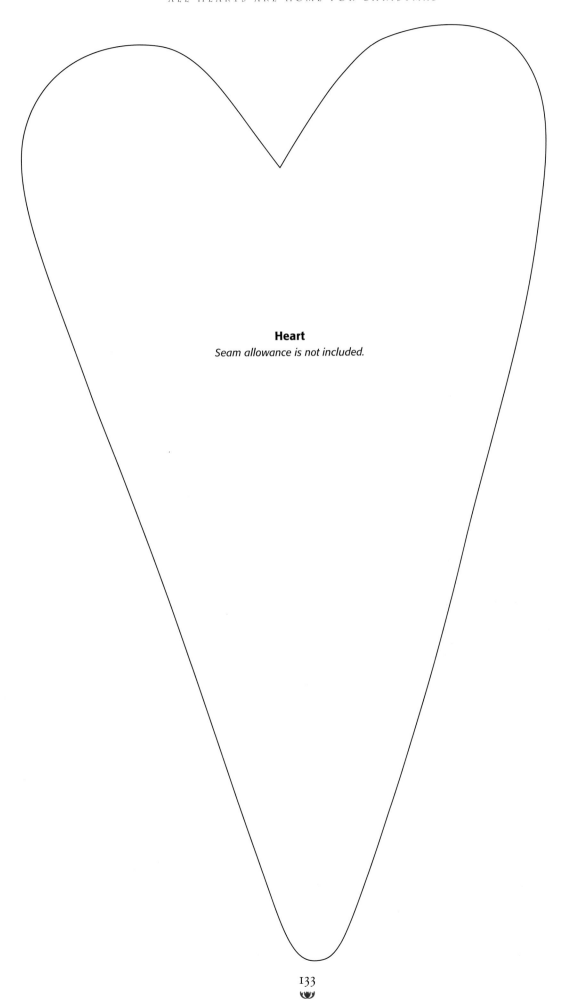

Heart
Seam allowance is not included.

A HEARTFELT CHRISTMAS

I have enjoyed Mary Hickey's friendship for a number of years, and I am always delighted to see her latest project. Mary is a talented designer and quiltmaker whose creativity knows no limits.

Mary and her husband, Phil, reside in their city house during the week, but they spend weekends (and as much other time as possible) at their beach house on Liberty Bay. It's hard to say whether the main attraction is the scenic location or their new granddaughter, Audrey, who lives nearby.

Mary's beach house makes a delightful setting for her two Christmas quilts. The beach house itself abounds with Mary's creativity, from gorgeous quilts to painted and stenciled furniture. Her books *The Joy of Quilting, The Simple Joys of Quilting* (both written with Joan Hanson), and *The Art of Stenciling* give ample testimony to Mary's abilities.

It's fun to visit Mary's design studio, a separate building that is just too cute for words. From the lace curtain stenciled on the window to the *trompe l'oeil* window painted on the exterior, Mary's studio showcases her artistry and how she uses it to solve what to some would be decorating dilemmas.

ABOVE: *Quilted Christmas stockings dangle from a mantel decorated with eye-catching Santas.*
OPPOSITE: *Two Christmas quilts jazz up the living room of Mary Hickey's beach house: "Wild Goose Chase" on the table and "Hidden Star and Christmas Hearts" on the sofa.*

WILD GOOSE CHASE

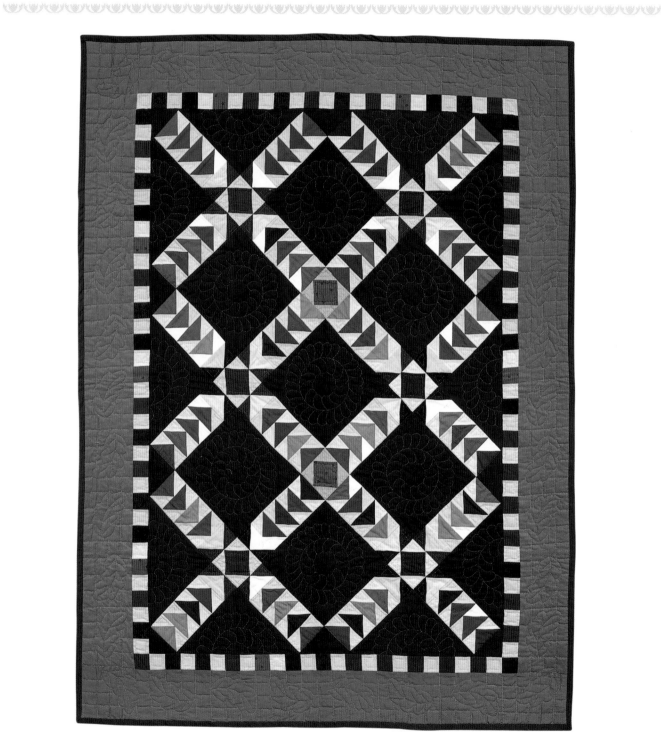

By Mary Hickey, Seattle, Washington, 2001. Quilted by Hazel Montague, Bellingham, Washington.
Finished quilt size: 40⅝" x 55⅝"; finished wild goose sections: 3" x 7½".

The name of this quilt always makes me think of my family chasing our old goose, Charlie, around the yard while trying to put him in the shed and out of a snowstorm. Of course, Charlie was smart enough to elude us but not bright enough to get in out of the ice. In the end, my son managed to scoop Charlie out of a cedar tree and save his delicate little goose feet from frostbite. Obviously, though, the name of this quilt really refers to geese flying in formation to reach their migration destinations.

Think of the wild goose sections as sashing and the background pieces as quilt blocks made of only one square. Simply cut the blocks 7½" square and they are finished! Then you can feel a little above average because you are making *pieced sashing*! Use the folded corner technique and include a variety of blues and greens for your geese sections to make your quilt really sparkle.

—MARY HICKEY

Materials

Yardages are based on 42"-wide fabrics unless otherwise noted.

- 1½ yds. green solid for outer border
- 1 yd. total assorted off-white solids for wild goose sections
- 1 yd. blue solid for blocks, setting triangles, and binding
- ⅝ yd. total assorted blues for wild goose sections
- ⅝ yd. total assorted greens for wild goose sections
- ½ yd. total assorted reds for wild goose sections and checked border
- ⅛ yd. gold for wild goose sections and checked border
- ⅛ yd. yellow for wild goose sections
- 2¾ yds. fabric for backing
- 47" x 62" batting

Cutting

From the off-white solids, cut:

- 2 strips, 2" x 42"; cut strips into 24 rectangles, 2" x 3½"
- 10 strips, 2" x 42"; cut strips into 192 squares, 2" x 2"
- 12 squares, 3" x 3"; cut squares once diagonally to make 24 triangles
- 3 strips, 1¾" x 42"

From the blue solid, cut:

- 2 strips, 8" x 42"; cut into 7 squares, 8" x 8"
- 3 squares, 12" x 12"; cut squares twice diagonally to make 12 large setting triangles
- 2 squares, 6" x 6"; cut squares twice diagonally to make 8 small setting triangles (you'll only need 6)

(Cutting is continued on the next page.)

From the blue solid, cut: (continued)

✦ 2 squares, 3½" x 3½"; cut squares once diagonally to make 4 corner triangles

NOTE: *The setting and corner triangles are cut slightly oversize. You can trim away any excess when squaring up the finished quilt top.*

From the assorted blues, cut:

✦ 3 strips, 3½" x 42"; cut strips into 48 rectangles, 2" x 3½"

From the assorted greens, cut:

✦ 3 strips, 3½" x 42"; cut strips into 48 rectangles, 2" x 3½"

From the green solid, cut on the lengthwise grain:

✦ 2 strips, 4½" x 47⅝"
✦ 2 strips, 4½" x 40¾"

From the assorted reds, cut:

✦ 2 strips, 2" x 42"; cut strips into 48 squares, 2" x 2"
✦ 6 squares, 3½" x 3½"
✦ 3 strips, 1¾" x 42"

From the gold, cut:

✦ 2 squares, 3½" x 3½"

From the yellow, cut:

✦ 4 squares, 3" x 3"; cut squares once diagonally to make 8 triangles

Making the Wild Geese Sections

1. Place a 2" off-white square on one end of a 2" x 3½" blue rectangle. Stitch a seam diagonally from one corner of the square to the other, as shown. Trim away the excess fabric from the corner, cutting ¼" away from the sewn line. Flip the resulting off-white triangle open and press. Repeat on the opposite end of the blue rectangle with another off-white square, being sure to stitch as shown to make a flying geese unit. Repeat to make a total of 96 blue and green flying geese units.

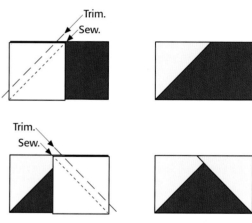

Make 96 blue and 96 green.

2. Using the 2" x 3½" off-white rectangles and the 2" red squares, make 24 red-and-white flying geese units.

Make 24.

3. Sew the flying geese units together in sets of five. Each segment should have a white-and-red unit at the top, followed by an assortment of four blue-and-white and green-and-white units. Make 24 of these segments.

Make 24.

Making the Square within a Square Sections

1. Stitch two 3" off-white triangles to each red square, as shown. Press the seam allowances toward the red squares.

2. Stitch two more off-white triangles to the red squares, as shown. Press the seam allowances toward the red squares.

Make 6.

3. In the same manner as steps 1 and 2, sew four 3" yellow triangles to the 3½" gold squares. Make two of these blocks.

Assembling the Quilt

1. Referring to the diagram below and the color photograph on page 136, arrange the flying geese sections, the Square-within-a-Square sections, and the large and small solid blue setting squares and triangles in diagonal rows.

2. Sew the blocks and segments together into rows. Press the seams toward the setting squares.

3. Join the rows together, and then add the blue corner triangles. Press all seams toward the setting pieces.

Adding the Pieced Border

IMPORTANT: The squares in this checkerboard border are cut at 1¾", which is just a little smaller than they need to be to fit the quilt top. They need to finish at 1⁵⁄₁₆" rather than the 1¼" they will be if you sew a full ¼" seam allowance. Since it's difficult to measure and cut the needed size with a rotary-cutting ruler, make the 1¾" squares fit your quilt by sewing the seams with a *scant ¼"* seam. That will make the checks slightly larger than 1¾". Sew just one border and try it on. If it doesn't fit properly, adjust one or two of the seam allowances until it does. Then make the necessary adjustments to your seam allowance when you sew the remaining borders.

1. Using a *scant ¼"* seam allowance, stitch the three off-white and three red 1¾" x 42" strips together into a strip set, alternating the colors. Cut the strip set into 1¾"-wide segments.

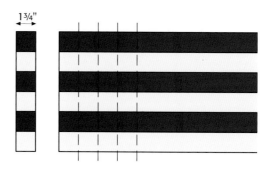

2. Still using a scant ¼" seam allowance, stitch the segments together to make long strips of alternating squares. You'll need two strips with 34 pieces in each for the side borders. These should start with white and end with red squares. You'll also need two strips with 25 pieces in each for the top and bottom borders. One of these strips should start and end with red squares. The other should start and end with white squares.

   If you prefer, you can randomly substitute 1¾" gold squares for some of the red ones.

3. Sew the long checked borders to the sides of the quilt top. Then sew the top and bottom borders to the quilt, making sure that the colors are lined up so that they continue the check pattern at the corners, referring to the quilt plan on page 141.

Used as a table topper, the "Wild Goose Chase" quilt coordinates perfectly with Mary's wooden house and trees.

Adding the Outer Border

1. Sew the 4½" x 47⅝" green outer border strips to the sides of the quilt. Press the seams toward the outer borders.

2. Sew the 4½" x 40¾" outer border strips to the top and bottom of the quilt. Press the seams toward the outer borders.

Finishing the Quilt

1. Piece the quilt backing so that it is approximately 6" larger than the quilt top. Layer the quilt top, batting, and backing, and baste, referring to "Layering and Basting" on page 155.

2. Hand or machine quilt as desired. The quilt shown is hand quilted with feathered wreaths in the dark blue setting squares and triangles. Leaves are quilted in the green outer border and are surrounded by a 1¼" grid that lines up with the inner checked border. The quilting stitches are white so they show up nicely on the dark solid fabrics.

3. Trim the excess batting and backing fabric from the quilt. If desired, add a hanging sleeve, referring to page 157 for details.

4. Cut strips to make 202" of straight-grain binding and attach it to the quilt, referring to "Binding" on page 157 for details.

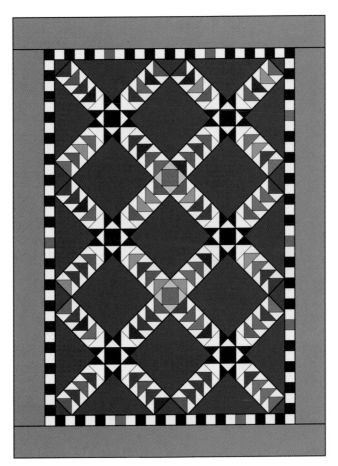

Quilt Plan

HIDDEN STAR
AND CHRISTMAS HEARTS

By Mary Hickey, Seattle, Washington, 2001. Quilted by Frankie Schmitt, Kenmore, Washington.
Finished quilt size: 48½" x 48½"; finished block size: 6".

What a lovely illusion! Create a star without making a Star block. Just make simple heart blocks with striped corners, and when you turn the heart blocks on-point and set them together, the stripes create the points of the star. Place a Square-within-a-Square block in the center of four Heart blocks, and the star magically appears. Use the folded corner technique to make the blocks, and you'll have this project finished in a heartbeat!

—MARY HICKEY

Materials

Yardages are based on 42"-wide fabrics unless otherwise noted.

- 1 yd. small-scale beige print for Heart blocks and borders
- 1 yd. (or scraps) of red for Heart blocks
- 1 yd. dark green 1 for outer border and binding
- ¾ yd. large-scale beige print for setting squares and triangles
- ⅝ yd. medium green for ribbon border
- ½ yd. green-and-beige stripe for Heart blocks
- ⅓ yd. dark green 2 for pieced border
- ¼ yd. light green for Square-within-a-Square blocks
- ¼ yd. medium-light green for Square-within-a-Square blocks
- 1½ yds. fabric for backing
- 53" x 53" batting

Cutting

From the small-scale beige print, cut:
- 3 strips, 1½" x 42"; cut strips into 64 squares, 1½" x 1½"
- 3 strips, 1½" x 42"; cut strips into 16 rectangles, 1½" x 6½"
- 4 strips, 2½" x 42"
- 5 strips, 2" x 42"
- 8 squares, 2½" x 2½"

From the large-scale beige print, cut:
- 5 squares, 6½" x 6½"
- 3 squares, 10½" x 10½"; cut squares twice diagonally to make 12 setting triangles
- 2 squares, 5½" x 5½; cut squares once diagonally to make 4 corner triangles

From the red fabrics, cut:
- 32 rectangles, 3½" x 5½"

From the green-and-beige stripe, cut:
- 32 squares, 3½" x 3½"

From the light green, cut:
- 16 squares, 3½" x 3½"

(Cutting is continued on the next page.)

From the medium-light green, cut:

✦ 4 squares, 6½" x 6½"

From the medium green, cut:

✦ 2 strips, 6½" x 42"; cut strips into 24 rectangles, 2½" x 6½"

✦ 2 squares, 3½" x 3½"

✦ 4 squares, 2½" x 2½"

From dark green 2, cut:

✦ 2 strips, 2½" x 42"

✦ 2 squares, 3½" x 3½"

From dark green 1, cut:

✦ 5 strips, 3½" x 42"

Making the Blocks

1. Use a pencil to lightly draw a diagonal line on the backs of the 1½" beige squares.

2. Lightly draw a diagonal line on the backs of the 3½" green-and-beige striped squares. Make sure that half of the blocks are marked with the diagonal going in one direction and the other half are marked in the opposite direction, as shown. Otherwise, some of your star points will have horizontal stripes rather than vertical stripes.

Make 16.   Make 16.

3. Place the squares, right sides together, on the red rectangles, and stitch as shown. Notice that 16 of the red rectangles should have the large triangle on the right side and 16 should have it on the left. Trim away the excess fabric from each corner, leaving a ¼" seam allowance. Press the triangles open.

Make 16.

Make 16.

In the corner by the Christmas tree is the perfect place to snuggle under a quilt while waiting for Santa.

4. Sew a 1½" beige square to each of the unsewn corners of the red rectangles in the same manner as you stitched the striped squares.

5. Sew the completed red rectangles together in pairs, making sure the green stripes are vertical on both sides. Sew a 1½" x 6½" small-scale beige strip to the top of each heart to complete 16 Heart blocks.

Heart Block
Make 16.

6. To make the Square-within-a-Square blocks, use a pencil to lightly draw diagonal lines on the backs of the 3½" light green squares. Place the squares face down on opposite corners of the 6½" medium-light green squares, and stitch as shown.

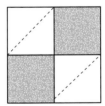

Trim the seam allowance to ¼" and press the triangles open. Place light green squares face down in the remaining corners and stitch, trim, and press as before. Repeat to make four blocks.

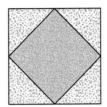

Square-within-a-Square Block
Make 4.

Assembling the Quilt Top

1. Referring to the diagram below and the quilt photograph on page 142, arrange the Heart blocks, the Square-within-a-Square blocks, the setting squares, and side and corner triangles in diagonal rows.

2. Sew the blocks together into rows. Press the seams toward the setting squares.

3. Sew the rows together and press the seams toward the setting pieces. Add the corner triangles and press.

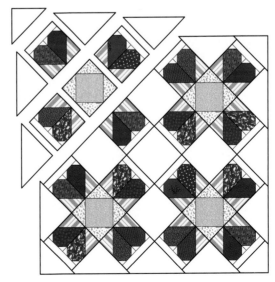

Quilt Assembly

Making the Pieced Border

1. Sew a 2½"-wide small-scale beige strip to either side of a 2½"-wide dark green 2 strip. Press the seams toward the green fabric. Repeat to make two strip sets. Cut the strip sets into twenty-four 2½"-wide segments.

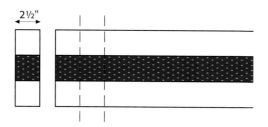

2. Staggering the pieces, stitch the beige-and-dark green segments to the 2½" x 6½" medium green segments. To align the pieces, the ends of the medium green segments should extend ¼" past the seam intersections of the beige and dark green seams in the strip-pieced segments. For the top and bottom borders, join six pieced segments and six medium green segments. Make sure that the medium green segments are angled from the bottom left to the upper right.

Make 2.

3. For the side borders, stagger the pieces as described in step 2 and join six pieced segments and six medium green segments, with the green segments angled from the bottom right to the top left, as shown.

Make 2.

4. Trim the jagged edges of all four borders. Align the ¼" line on your rotary-cutting ruler with the points where the medium and dark green fabrics intersect to allow for a ¼" seam allowance on each side of the borders.

Make 2.

5. To complete the ribbon turns at each corner, you'll need to make two different types of corner blocks. Using the folded corner technique as you did for the Heart blocks, sew two 2½" beige squares to opposite corners of a 3½" dark green square. Sew two medium green 2½" squares to the other corners of the block and trim the excess fabric on all four corners. Press the block and repeat to make two corner blocks.

Make 2.

6. For the other corner blocks, sew two 2½" beige squares to opposite sides of a 3½" medium green square. Trim the corners and press the block. Repeat to make two.

Make 2.

7. Sew the corner blocks to the top and bottom borders, paying close attention to the color placement so that the ribbon design twists at each corner, as shown. Attach the borders to the quilt, referring to the quilt plan below.

Adding the Outer Borders

1. To make the middle border, measure the length of your quilt top through the center and trim two of the 2" wide beige strips to this length. Sew the borders to the sides of the quilt and press the seams toward the beige fabric.

2. Sew the remaining three 2"-wide beige strips together end to end. Measure the width of your quilt top through the center and cut two borders to this length from the long strip. Sew the borders to the top and bottom of the quilt, and press the seams toward the beige fabric.

Quilt Plan

3. To make the outer border, cut one of the 3"-wide dark green 1 strips into four equal lengths. Sew one of these pieces to each of the four remaining 42"-long strips. Measure the length of the quilt through the center and trim two of the border strips to this length. Sew the borders to the sides of the quilt. Repeat, measuring the width of the quilt through the center and trimming the borders to fit. Press all the seams toward the green borders.

Finishing the Quilt

1. Trim the quilt backing so that it is approximately 6" larger than the quilt top. Layer the quilt top, batting, and backing, and baste, referring to "Layering and Basting" on page 155.

2. Hand or machine quilt as desired. The quilt shown was machine quilted with echo quilting in the hearts and center squares of the stars. The pieced border is outline quilted, and the background areas are all meander quilted.

3. Trim the excess batting and backing fabric from the quilt. If desired, add a hanging sleeve, referring to page 157 for details.

4. Make and attach straight-grain binding, referring to "Binding" on page 157 for details.

The "Hidden Star and Christmas Hearts" quilt introduces a splash of color to the dark blue sofa and Liberty Bay vista beyond.

QUILTMAKING BASICS

In this section, you'll find tips for completing a quilt with confidence and pride. What I suggest works well for me, but it is by no means the only way to accomplish the job. If a technique is new to you, try it; you might find that you incorporate it into your quiltmaking process from now on.

Bias Squares

Many quilt patterns contain squares made from two contrasting half-square triangles. The short sides of the triangles are on the straight grain of the fabric, while the long sides are on the bias. These are called bias squares. Using a bias-strip piecing method, you can easily sew and cut bias squares. This technique is especially useful for small bias squares, where pressing after stitching can distort the shape (and sometimes burn fingers). An easy way to cut bias squares for a scrappy-quilt look is to use 7" or 8" squares of fabric. For quilts with bias squares that are all cut from the same fabrics, use larger pieces. Measurements are included in the quilt directions.

NOTE: *All directions in this book give the cut size for bias squares; the finished size after stitching will be ½" smaller.*

1. Layer both pieces of fabric called for in the project directions with right sides facing up. Whether you're starting with squares or rectangles of fabric, make a 45° diagonal cut beginning in one corner.

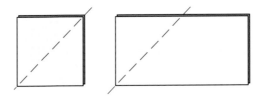

2. Cut the layered fabrics into strips, measuring from the previous diagonal cut. (The width to cut the bias strips is included in the individual project directions.)

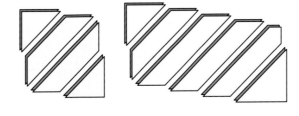

3. Stitch the strips together, alternating the two fabrics and using ¼" seam allowances. While the strips will be various lengths, align them so that they form a straight edge along the bottom of the patchwork and right angles at the bottom corners. Sew the triangles cut from the corners to the upper left and bottom right corners of the assembled strips. Press seams toward the darker fabric.

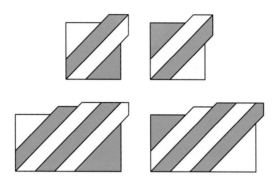

4. Begin cutting at the lower left corner. Align the 45° mark of a Bias Square® ruler on the seam line. Each bias square will require four cuts. The first and second cuts are along the side and top edge. They remove the bias square from the rest of the

fabric. Make these cuts slightly larger than the correct size.

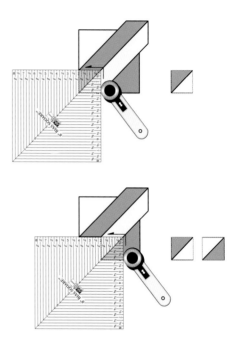

Align 45° mark on seam line and cut first 2 sides.

5. The third and fourth cuts are made along the remaining two sides. They align the diagonal and trim the bias square to the correct size. To make these cuts, turn the segment and place the Bias Square ruler on the opposite two sides, aligning the required measurements on both sides of the cutting guide and the 45° mark on the seam. Cut the remaining two sides of the bias squares.

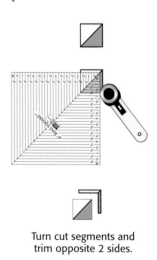

Turn cut segments and
trim opposite 2 sides.

6. Continue cutting bias squares from each unit in this manner, working from left to right and from bottom to top, until you have cut bias squares from all usable fabric.

Bias Rectangles

Making bias rectangles is similar to making bias squares, but you will need a BiRangle® ruler, rather than a Bias Square ruler, for this technique.

1. Layer both fabrics specified in the project directions *face down* on the cutting mat.

2. Fold the fabrics in half, selvage to selvage (the way they are folded on the bolt). Cutting strips with the fabrics folded creates mirror-image rectangles, which are needed for most projects using bias rectangles.

3. Place the fold on the right. Place the BiRangle ruler on the edge of the fabrics, with the long side on the selvages.

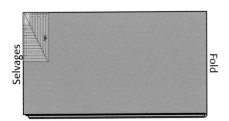

4. Place a large cutting ruler on the diagonal line of the BiRangle, as shown, and then carefully slide the BiRangle out of the way. Cut along the edge of the ruler.

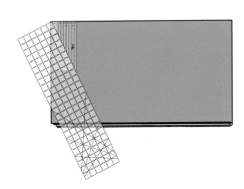

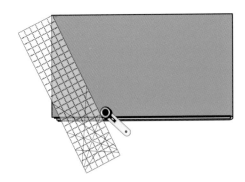

5. Cut strips parallel to the first cut. Each quilt project will specify how wide to cut the bias strips. The two large triangles aren't needed, so you can put them in your scrap basket.

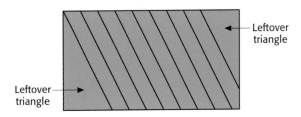

6. Sort the strips into two sets, ones that slant left and ones that slant right. Set aside the strips that slant to the right for now so that you don't get them mixed up.

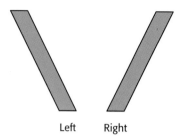

Left   Right

7. Arrange the left-slanting strips in a unit, alternating the colors. Place the odd-shaped strips at the ends of the unit. The tops of the strips should form a straight line.

8. Sew the strips together in pairs, offsetting the tops of the strips ¼" before stitching the seam. Sew the pairs into a unit, again offsetting the strips ¼" at the top. Finally, sew the odd-shaped strips to the ends of the unit, as shown. Press the seams toward the darker fabric.

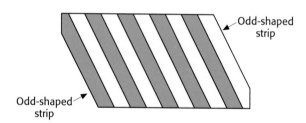

Odd-shaped strip

Odd-shaped strip

9. Place the assembled fabric on the cutting mat. You might need to angle it for a better fit. Place the BiRangle over the fabric so that the diagonal line on the ruler is on top of the seam line closest to the bottom right corner of the fabric. Slide the ruler until the measurement specified in your

project directions is completely over the fabric.

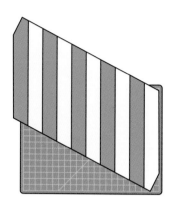

10. Cut along the top and left edges of the BiRangle to separate the oversize bias rectangle from the rest of the fabric. Then turn the cut piece over, place the diagonal line along the stitching line, and slide the ruler until the exact measurement you need is even with the already-cut edges. Trim away the excess fabric from the remaining two sides of the rectangle.

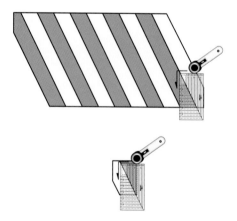

11. Continue cutting one rectangle at a time in the same manner as described in steps 9 and 10.

12. Work your way across a horizontal row of the fabric. If more bias rectangles are needed, begin cutting them from the bottom right corner of the assembled fabric.

13. Piece the right-slanting strips together in the same manner as you did the left-slanting strips. To make the finished pieces easier to sew together, try pressing the seams on this unit toward the lighter fabric.

Cutting Motif Fabric

When using a fabric with a large theme print, such as the Dick and Jane flannel fabric shown on page 102, you'll want to center the motif in the patches you're cutting. An easy way to do this is to cut a piece of clear template plastic to the cut size (including seam allowances) of the square or other shape you need to cut. Draw diagonal lines from each corner to the opposite corner, and where the lines intersect is the center of the template. Place the template over the fabric and move it around until you have the motif centered under the plastic.

To cut the fabric, either carefully lay your ruler along one edge of the template and use a rotary cutter to cut the fabric. Do this for each edge, taking care not to move the template. Or use a pencil or chalk wheel to mark around the template, and then remove it and cut the fabric on the marked lines.

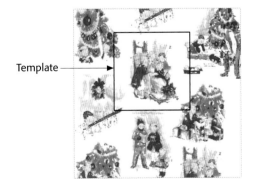

Template →

Fusible Appliqué

Fusible appliqué is a time-saving technique that allows you to appliqué in a fraction of the time required for more traditional methods. Some of the projects in this book have instructions calling specifically for fusible appliqué, but with a little preplanning, any of the appliqué patterns in this book can be adapted to the fusible technique. Follow the manufacturer's instructions carefully when using fusible web. It's best to reserve fusible appliqués for small accents or to secure the edges with stitching (see step 5 on page 154) if you plan to launder the quilt.

1. Prepare the pieces for appliqué by tracing the shapes onto the paper side of the fusible web. Patterns designed specifically for fusible-web appliqué have already been reversed. If you are adapting a pattern intended for hand appliqué, you'll need to reverse the pattern before tracing.

2. Using a dry (no steam) iron, follow the manufacturer's instructions and fuse the webbing to the wrong side of the fabric.

3. Cut on the drawn line and remove the paper backing.

4. Fuse the pieces to the background block or border.

5. To secure the appliqués more permanently to the fabric, finish the edges with hand or machine blanket stitch.

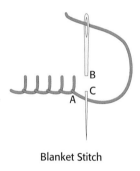

Blanket Stitch

Mitered Corners

1. To find the border length of the sides of the quilt, measure through the center of the quilt top from the top edge to the bottom edge. Add two times the border width (included in quilt directions) to this measurement; then add 2" to 3" extra to allow for the mitered corner's 45° angle. Repeat to find the border length for the top and bottom of the quilt by measuring through the center of the quilt horizontally, and cut borders to these measurements. If

multiple border strips are planned, piece these together into a border unit.

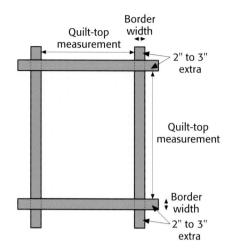

2. For one side of the quilt top, fold a border strip in half to find the center. Match the center of the border strip to the center of the edge on the quilt top. Pin the border in place, and start and end stitching ¼" from each corner of the quilt top. Repeat for the remaining three sides.

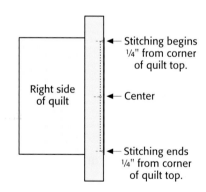

3. Arrange a corner of the quilt on an ironing board, crossing one border over the other at a 90° angle.

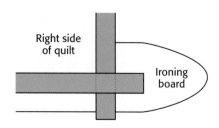

4. Turn under the overlapping (top) border, making a 45°-angle fold; press. This is the stitching line.

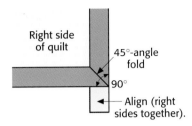

5. Fold the quilt, right sides together, matching borders at the corner. Pin to secure. Stitch on the pressed crease, backstitching at the outside edge and corner. Take care to keep the seam allowances out of the way.

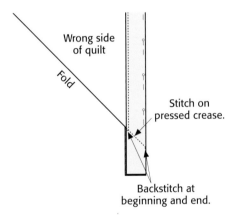

6. Trim the mitered seam allowances to ¼"; press seam open flat. Repeat for the remaining corners.

Quilt Backing

If your quilt top is wider than 42", you will need to piece the back, although occasionally you can find extra-wide fabric. For large quilts, you might need to sew two or three lengths of fabric together to make the backing large enough. Press the seams open; quilting through them can be difficult.

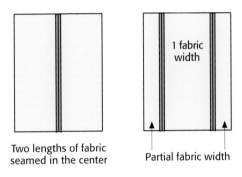

Two lengths of fabric seamed in the center

Partial fabric width

When choosing a fabric for your quilt backing, remember that solids or subtle prints show off your quilting stitches, while busy prints tend to hide them. The yardage requirements for each project allow enough fabric so that quilt backings can be at least 6" larger than bed-size quilt tops and at least 4" larger than wall-hanging quilt tops.

Layering and Basting

Before you quilt your layers together, baste them. You will find that a good basting job allows you to use any method of quilting with which you are comfortable. To baste the layers, first press the backing. Place it wrong side up on a large table or other clean, flat surface. Secure the backing with masking tape or clips, gently pulling the fabric so that it lies taut but not stretched. Center a piece of batting over the backing and smooth out any wrinkles. Finish the "sandwich" by centering the quilt top right side up over the two layers.

Pin through all layers to secure, if desired. With a contrasting-color thread, baste a square grid from the center out, in rows placed a maximum of 3" apart. (Baste only the portion of the quilt that lies on the table surface, and reposition the quilt as needed to baste the other areas.) Take long running stitches until you reach the end of the grid; then take a backstitch and remove the needle.

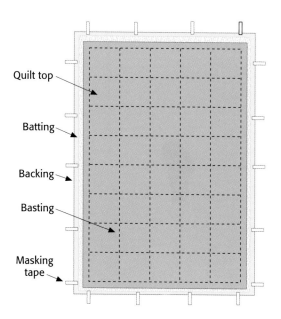

Quilt top

Batting

Backing

Basting

Masking tape

Hand Quilting

Once you have basted your quilt layers, you are ready to quilt. You may use a hoop or a frame to support your work and keep it taut. If you prefer, you may simply quilt in your lap. Experiment to find the method you prefer.

1. Choose a sturdy needle (a size 10 Between, for example), 100 percent–cotton quilting thread, and a thimble for the middle finger of your quilting hand. Cut an 18" length of thread, thread the needle, and make a small knot at the end of the thread.

2. Work from the center of the quilt outward. Insert the needle through the quilt top, running it between the layers about 1" from where you plan to begin stitching. Bring the needle out on the stitching line and tug gently on the thread to pull the knot between the layers.

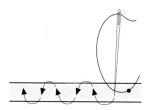

3. Take a small backstitch through all three layers; then take small, even running stitches—two or three at a time—rocking the needle up and down with each stitch. Keep your other hand underneath the quilt, feeling the needle go through the layers and pushing it back up. Remove basting threads as you go.

4. When you near the end of the length of thread, make a knot close to your work. Insert the needle into the hole where it last emerged, and slide it between the layers for approximately 1", bringing it out on top. Gently pull the knot inside the layers. Carefully clip the remaining thread tail close to the quilt top.

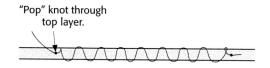

"Pop" knot through top layer.

Hanging Sleeve

If you plan to hang your quilt, attach a sleeve to the back before attaching the binding. From the leftover backing fabric, cut an 8"-wide strip of fabric equal to the width of your quilt. (You might need to piece two or three strips together for larger quilts.) On each end of the strip, fold over ½" and then fold ½" again. Press and stitch in place by machine.

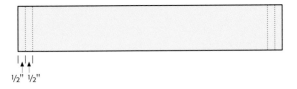

½" ½"

Fold the strip in half lengthwise, wrong sides together, and baste the raw edges of the sleeve to the top edge of the back of your quilt. These edges will be secured when you sew on the binding. After the binding is applied, slip-stitch the ends and bottom of the sleeve to the quilt backing, making a little pleat in the sleeve to accommodate the thickness of the rod.

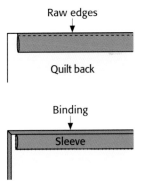

Raw edges

Quilt back

Binding

Sleeve

Binding

Many of the quilts in this book call for double-fold binding made from 2¼"-wide bias strips. Others use straight-grain binding. The quilt directions tell you how much fabric and how many inches of binding you will need to bind the perimeter of your quilt.

After quilting, trim the excess batting and backing even with the edge of the quilt top. A rotary cutter and a long ruler will ensure accurate, straight edges. Baste all three layers together along the outside edges. (If you have a walking foot, you can do this with a longer-than-normal stitch on your sewing machine.)

CUTTING STRAIGHT-GRAIN BINDING

For straight-grain, double-fold binding, cut strips 2" to 2½" wide across the width of the fabric. You will need enough strips to go around the perimeter of the quilt plus 10" for seams and to turn the corners.

CUTTING BIAS BINDING

1. Align the 45° mark of a Bias Square ruler along the selvage and place a long ruler's edge against it. Make the first cut.

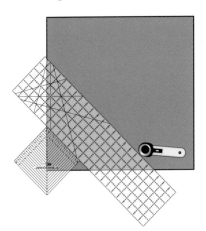

2. Measure the width of the strip (2¼") from the cut edge of the fabric. Cut along the edge with the ruler. Continue cutting until you have the number of strips necessary to achieve the required binding length.

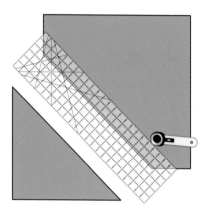

3. Sometimes a 24"-long ruler may be too short for some of the cuts. After making several cuts, carefully fold the fabric over itself so that the bias edges are even. Continue to cut the bias strips.

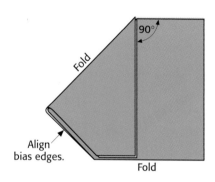

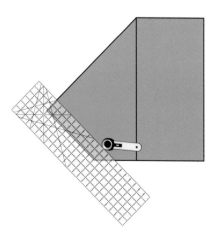

ATTACHING BINDING

1. With right sides together, join strips at right angles and stitch across the corner as shown. Trim excess fabric and press the seams open to make one long piece of binding.

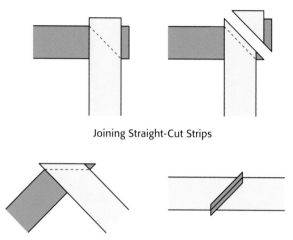

Joining Straight-Cut Strips

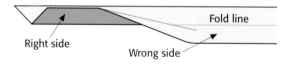

2. Fold the strip in half lengthwise, wrong sides together, and press.

3. Unfold the binding at one end and turn under ¼" at a 45° angle, as shown. Refold the binding after turning the end under.

4. Starting on one side of the quilt (not at a corner), stitch the binding to the quilt. Use a ¼" seam allowance. Begin stitching 1" to 2" from the start of the binding. Stop stitching ¼" from the first corner and backstitch.

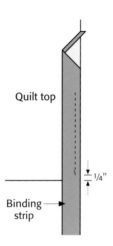

5. Turn the quilt to prepare for sewing along the next edge. Fold the binding away from the quilt; then fold the binding again to place it along the second edge of the quilt. This fold creates an angled pleat at the corner.

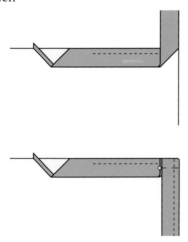

6. Stitch from the fold of the binding along the second edge of the quilt top, stopping ¼" from the corner as before. Repeat the stitching and mitering process on the remaining edges and corners of the quilt.

7. When you reach the beginning of the binding, cut the end 1" longer than needed, and tuck the end inside the beginning. Finish stitching the binding to the quilt.

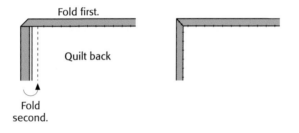

8. Turn the binding over the raw edges to the back side of the quilt. Blindstitch the binding in place so that the folded edge covers the machine stitching. Fold the binding at each corner to form a miter on the back of the quilt, and stitch in place.

QUILT RESOURCE LIST

I AM FORTUNATE to have a large number of quilts with which to decorate. These include my antique quilt collection along with myriad quilts designed for my books. Since I have written more than 30 quilting titles over the past 20 years, I have a wealth of quilts to display in my home and feature in the photos of this book.

There was not enough space to give directions for making all the quilts shown in this book, so I am providing this list of books published by Martingale & Company/That Patchwork Place where you can find directions for other quilts you may want to make.

The first number in each entry refers to the page in this book where the quilt is pictured. The quilt name and the title and author of the book in which it originally appeared are then given. The number in parentheses refers to the page in that book on which directions can be found. Books that are no longer in print are indicated by an asterisk (*); you may be able to find them in public or quilt guild libraries.

Page 6: Antique "Pine Burr" quilt hung over cupboard door: no pattern available.

Page 9: "St. Benedict's Star," *Angle Antics** by Mary Hickey (page 28).

Page 13: Antique quilts on bench: no patterns available.

Page 25: "Feathered World without End," *Classic Quilts with Precise Foundation Piecing** by Tricia Lund and Judy Pollard (page 44).

Page 32: "Lost Ships" signature quilt, *Rotary Riot** by Judy Hopkins and Nancy J. Martin (page 24).

Page 39: "Rose Wreath," *Make Room for Quilts* by Nancy J. Martin (page 200).

Page 42: "Kitty Homemaker," *Kitties to Stitch and Quilt* by Nancy J. Martin (page 25).

Page 48: "Tree of Life," *Two-Color Quilts* by Nancy J. Martin (page 37).

Page 53: "Christmas Nine Patch," *Time-Crunch Quilts* by Nancy J. Martin (page 32).

Page 78: "Red Toile Double Irish Chain" on bed: no pattern available.

Page 79: "Lady of the Lake," *Back to Square One** by Nancy J. Martin (page 24).

Page 79: "Double Nine Patch" and "Cake Stand," *Two-Color Quilts* by Nancy J. Martin (pages 12 and 26, respectively).

Page 79: "Wonderful World," *Simply Scrappy Quilts** by Nancy J. Martin (page 38).

Page 84: "Winter Wonderland" on wall, *Home for Christmas** by Nancy J. Martin and Sharon Stanley (page 60).

Page 94: "Family Reunion" table runner by Mary V. Green, *Favorite Christmas Quilts from That Patchwork Place* (page 68).

Page 98: Double Nine Patch quilt top: no pattern available.

Page 98: "Burgoyne Surrounded," *Threads of Time** by Nancy J. Martin (page 134).

Page 100: "Norway Pine," *Time-Crunch Quilts* by Nancy J. Martin (page 48).

Page 100: "House" quilt, block pattern available in "Dream House" quilt, *Patchwork Picnic* by Suzette Halferty and Nancy J. Martin (page 106).

Page 110: "Homecoming Wreath," *Little Quilts All through the House* by Alice Berg, Sylvia Johnson, and Mary Ellen Von Holt (page 64).

Page 110: "Cake Stand," *Time-Crunch Quilts* by Nancy J. Martin (page 36).

Page 118: Antique quilts: no patterns available.

Page 123: Sampler quilt: no pattern available.

Page 126: "My Favorite Things," *Folk Art Quilts: A Fresh Look* by Sandy Bonsib (page 36).

Page 126: "Color Me Bright," *Folk Art Quilts: A Fresh Look* by Sandy Bonsib (page 58).